PLACE IN RETURN BOX to remove this checkout from your record.
TO AVOID FINES return on or before date due.

DATE DUE	DATE DUE	DATE DUE
_____	_____	_____
_____	_____	_____
_____	_____	_____
_____	_____	_____
_____	_____	_____
_____	_____	_____
_____	_____	_____

MSU Is An Affirmative Action/Equal Opportunity Institution

Artisans

in Economic
Development

Evidence from Asia

Elwood A. Pye, editor

The International Development Research Centre is a public corporation created by the Parliament of Canada in 1970 to support research designed to adapt science and technology to the needs of developing countries. The Centre's activity is concentrated in six sectors: agriculture, food and nutrition sciences; health sciences; information sciences; social sciences; earth and engineering sciences; and communications. IDRC is financed solely by the Parliament of Canada; its policies, however, are set by an international Board of Governors. The Centre's headquarters are in Ottawa, Canada. Regional offices are located in Africa, Asia, Latin America, and the Middle East.

IDRC-262e

Artisans
in Economic Development

Evidence from Asia

Elwood A. Pye, editor

© International Development Research Centre 1988
Postal Address: Box 8500, Ottawa, Ont., Canada K1G 3H9

Pye, E.A., editor
                                                                IDRC-262e
    Artisans in Economic Development : Evidence from Asia. Ottawa, Ont.
IDRC, 1988. x + 125 p. : ill.

    /Handicrafts/, /craftsmen/, /employment/, /income/, /Asia/ - /industrial
production/,/household income/, /cottage industry/, /industrial promotion/,
/market/, /exports/, /foreign exchange/, /state participation/, /employment
creation/, /supply and demand/, /economic behaviour/, /surveys/, /case
studies/.

UDC: 331-057(5)   ISBN: 0-88936-508-3

Technical editor: S.D. Garland

A microfiche edition is available.

This work was carried out with the aid of a grant from the International
Development Research Centre, Ottawa, Canada. The views expressed are
those of the contributors and do not necessarily reflect the views of the
Centre.

Abstract

This book provides a detailed examination of the large and heterogeneous group of workers employed as artisans. Despite the size of this work force in Asia, artisans have rarely been the subject of development-oriented research. Rapid growth of exports and competition from factory products are forcing fundamental changes on a sector that has traditionally been responsible for creating millions of new jobs and earning a large amount in foreign exchange. Research into recent changes in this sector was carried out in Nepal, Sri Lanka, India, Malaysia, Indonesia, Thailand, and the Philippines. Economists and other social scientists looked at a comprehensive set of supply and demand issues, as well as government institutions and programs providing support. Key policy options for each country are discussed, with a view to determining how craft industries can remain viable in the future.

Résumé

Cet ouvrage étudie en profondeur le groupe considérable et hétérogène des travailleurs employés à titre d'artisans. Malgré l'importance de cette tranche de la main-d'oeuvre en Asie, les artisans ont rarement fait l'objet de recherches reliées au développement. La croissance rapide des exportations et la concurrence des produits de fabrication industrielle imposent des transformations fondamentales à un secteur traditionnelle-ment générateur de millions de nouveaux emplois et source importante de devises. Des recherches sur les changements récents qui se produisent dans ce secteur ont été réalisées au Népal, à Sri Lanka, en Inde, en Malaisie, en Indonésie, en Thaïlande et aux Philippines. Des économistes et d'autres spécialistes en sciences sociales ont examiné un éventail complet de problèmes reliés à l'offre et à la demande et se sont penchés sur les institutions et les programmes gouvernementaux de soutien. On aborde également les choix clés qui se présentent à chaque pays en matière de politique pour assurer la viabilité à long terme des industries artisanales.

Resumen

Este libro brinda un examen detallado del grande y heterogéneo grupo de trabajadores empleados como artesanos. A pesar de lo numerosa que es esta fuerza laboral en Asia, los artesanos han sido pocas veces objeto de investigaciones que hagan énfasis en el tema del desarrollo. Un rápido crecimiento de las exportaciones y la competencia que representan los productos elaborados en las fábricas, están creando forzosamente cambios fundamentales en un sector que por tradicin ha generado millones de nuevos puestos de trabajo y grandes cantidades de divisas extranjeras. La investigacin sobre cambios recientes en este sector se llev a cabo en Nepal, Sri Lanka, India, Malaysia, Indonesia, Thailand y Las Filipinas. Economistas y cientficos sociales de otros campos analizaron un amplio conjunto de cuestiones relacionadas con la oferta y la demanda, as como también instituciones y programas gubernamentales que proporcionan ayuda. Se discuten opciones principales de poltica para cada pas, con vistas a determinar el modo de mantener en pie a las industrias artesanales en el futuro.

Contributors

L.C. Jain, Industrial Development Services, New Delhi, India

Sanjay Kathuria, Indian Council for Research on International Economic Relations, New Delhi, India

Loekman Soetrisno and Rebecca Joseph, Research Centre for Rural and Regional Studies, Gadjah Mada University, Yogjakarta, Indonesia

Gusti N. Bagus and Wayan Tjatera, Udayana University, Denpasar, Indonesia

Kiran Upadhyay and Shiva Sharma, Tribhuvan University, Kirtipur, Nepal

Raja Fuziah, Malaysian Handicrafts Development Corporation, and Ismail Rejab, Universiti Kebangsaan Malaysia, Kuala Lumpur, Malaysia

Filomeno Aguilar and Virginia Miralao, Ramon Magsaysay Award Foundation, Manila, Philippines

Sunimal Fernando, Marga Institute, Colombo, Sri Lanka

Chaiwat Roongruangsee, Somnai Premchit, and Songsak Sriboonchitta, University of Chiangmai, Thailand

Contents

Foreword

This book was written in response to the almost total lack of information on Asia's artisans. Although these workers, and the overall sector, have been the subject of some review in India, this is not the case in the other six countries discussed here. Aside from occasional case studies, no socioeconomic data have been available for planning or reference.

This is surprising considering the economic contributions by these industries in terms of new employment and foreign exchange. Two examples from India, where time series data are available, illustrate this point. During 1961–81, the number of new jobs in crafts was comparable to that created by all private and public firms in the organized sectors combined. In trade, the Indian data show that, during 1978–79, earnings from artisan exports were greater than the total of all foreign aid receipts. These products now represent 16% of India's total trade and 13% of Nepal's. Such statistics are even more surprising when one considers how little financial support the industry receives. To date, artisans have given a great deal, but received little in return. This is no doubt one reason why many small producers are now in difficulty, largely as a result of falling demand brought about by factory competition. When these jobs are lost, it is unlikely that other employment will be available.

In response to this lack of information, and at the request of governments in the region, IDRC funded a seven-country research network on artisan industries in south and Southeast Asia during 1983–86. Research teams comprised economists, anthropologists, and marketing specialists. Each team worked in conjunction with central government agencies in trade, industry, and rural development. Separate questionnaires were given to producers, raw material suppliers, middlemen, and policymakers. In each country, industries that make products for local consumption, for tourists, and for export were selected, so that different market characteristics could be studied.

An analysis of the data from 23 industries has led to some interesting conclusions. Families involved in craft production are not only above the poverty line, but also have incomes over the national household average. In some countries, household incomes are many times higher. This reflects the strong export demand, but is also the result of multiple sources of family income for rural producers.

Despite these higher than expected earnings, returns to labour are very low and, partially as a result, an insufficient number of young people are entering the trade. In Malaysia and Sri Lanka, for example, the average age of an artisan is now over 40.

For this sector to survive, especially in the more developed Southeast Asian countries, government policies must emphasize exports. Wages are higher and benefits are more readily available in factories, which cater to exports. Furthermore, policymakers will find that the returns are good. For example, craft exports have increased four times faster than overall trade. What remains to be done, however, is to share these gains more equitably with producers. In doing so, this sector may be able to attract new workers.

This book is the first available in Asia, outside of India, on the economic conditions of this industry. It is our hope that this publication will be useful to government and nongovernment planners, other international agencies, and researchers who may wish to use this as a guide for their own work.

Anne Whyte
Director
Social Sciences Division
IDRC

Acknowledgments

This book is an analysis of primary data collected by researchers in seven countries during 1983–86, often under arduous and difficult circumstances. As such, my first debt is to them. The research coordinators of this program were: L.C. Jain, Industrial Development Services, and Sanjay Kathuria, Indian Council for Research on International Economic Relations, New Delhi, India; Loekman Soetrisno and Rebecca Joseph, Research Centre for Rural and Regional Studies, Gadjah Mada University, Yogjakarta, Indonesia; Gusti N. Bagus and Wayan Tjatera, Udayana University, Denpasar, Indonesia; Kiran Upadhyay and Shiva Sharma, Tribhuvan University, Kirtipur, Nepal; Raja Fuziah, Malaysian Handicrafts Development Corporation, and Ismail Rejab, Universiti Kebangsaan Malaysia, Kuala Lumpur, Malaysia; Filomeno Aguilar and Virginia Miralao, Ramon Magsaysay Award Foundation, Manila, Philippines; Sunimal Fernando, Marga Institute, Colombo, Sri Lanka; and Chaiwat Roongruangsee, Somnai Premchit, and Songsak Sriboonchitta, University of Chiangmai, Thailand.

A considerable obligation is due to L.C. Jain, who also served as adviser to this program. His knowledge of this sector was fundamental in overcoming our lack of applied experience when this program first began. Among numerous other assignments, Mr Jain was a member of the All India Handicraft Board (1955–77), Chairman of this Board (1978–80), Director of the Handicrafts and Handlooms Corporation (1955–77), a member of the National Planning Commission's Steering Group on Employment Strategies for the Seventh Plan, and a member of the Advisory Board, Small Industry Development Bank of India.

I am obliged to the International Development Research Centre (IDRC) and its staff in Ottawa and Singapore for funding this program and for sustaining support over a long period of time. In particular, I would like to recognize David Glover, David King, and François Belisle from the Economic and Urban Policy Programs. In Singapore, where this program was managed, Jingjai Hanchanlash administered funds, Tan Say Yin assumed a heavy administrative load, and Veronica Ng spent countless hours revising the manuscript.

I appreciate the assistance of the International Labour Organization (ILO) in Geneva. The ILO provided me with excellent logistic and intellectual support during a sabbatical in 1986, at which time this manuscript was written. I would particularly like to acknowledge Stijin Albregts of ILO's Small Enterprise Development Program.

A word is in order on the authorship of the various chapters. The editor is responsible for the overview and regional chapters, and would like to acknowledge Hector Namay of the Ramon Magsaysay Award Foundation Research Group in Manila for his assistance in compiling the numerous tables. In addition, Virginia Miralao,

Research Project Head of this foundation, provided me with information and other support while I was in Geneva. The country reports were, for the most part, derived from studies put together by the researchers listed above. Because members of this network met on numerous occasions to review each other's work, in a real sense there is also a collective authorship. The editor was responsible for writing the reports for Nepal, Sri Lanka, Thailand, and Malaysia; the chapters for India and the Philippines are essentially the work of L.C. Jain and of Virginia Miralao and Filomeno Aguilar, respectively. Four case studies, which were originally part of this work, are published separately, by IDRC, under the title Artisan Industries in Asia: Four Case Studies (TS60e).

An Introduction and Overview

This publication represents 3 years of research by a dedicated group of economists and social scientists, who covered an area rarely looked at by their peers. The first two chapters introduce the material and draw it together as a regional synthesis. Detailed country reports then follow. Case studies on topics, such as labour conditions and export policies, which are important to this industry and which formed part of this research project, may be found in a companion publication called *Artisan Industries in Asia: Four Case Studies* (Kathuria et al. 1988).

The industries studied in this research program vary in terms of their resource endowments and markets. Some are rural based and produce goods for local domestic use. Others are located in cities and towns and cater to the tourist and export markets. However, there is one common feature: all represent products that require some degree of artistic skill. This feature separates the group of industries studied here from other informal sector enterprises or other small and medium-sized firms. For example, issues relating to the transfer of skills and the use of technology assume greater importance. Furthermore, these products are widely traded, a feature which is not common to other goods made by small enterprises. In short, policy measures for supporting these industries will differ to some considerable extent from those that are applied to the small-scale industrial sector in general.

In Asia, the terms artisan and craftsperson are synonymous and refer to workers who apply some degree of artistic skill to the products they make. As such, the terms have a different meaning than in Latin America or Africa, where they are used to represent a much broader group of workers. In Africa, for example, it is common to use the term artisan to describe almost anyone who works in an informal sector enterprise. This is not the case in Asia.

With numerous exceptions, the following characteristics can be loosely applied to the industries studied here: competitive markets, diversified market structure, high labour intensity, low capital requirements, some artistic skill, small scale of production, simple technologies, and the use of local raw materials. However, the exceptions should also be noted. Capital requirements for purchasing raw materials are very high in some industries, particularly export-oriented ones, because materials are often imported. Furthermore, as a result of exports, production may not be small and often utilizes factory modes. In some cases, the technology has become sophisticated enough to be considered a trade secret.

Scope of the Study

Industries making the following products were studied in seven countries:

India	carpets, metal, wood, stone, embroidery, gems
Indonesia[a]	textiles, metal, wood
Nepal	metal, wood, cotton, wool textiles
Malaysia	metal, textiles, forest-based products
Philippines	rattan, cotton textiles, embroidery, forest-based products
Sri Lanka	brass, pottery
Thailand	wood, wicker, cotton textiles

[a] Due to data collection problems, much of this information was deleted from the tables in this publication. However, reliable information on the batik industry has been included in Kathuria et al. (1988).

In each industry, separate questionnaires were administered to artisans, raw material suppliers, marketing agents, and policymakers. The sample sizes can be found in each country report. In some cases, one person may perform more than one function, such as artisans who supply their own materials and market the final product. However, subcontracting is prevalent throughout the region, so there is often a fairly clear division of labour.

Research covered the three major markets to which artisans cater: local domestic consumption, tourists, and exports. This allowed us to study different market responses as well as production problems unique to each market.

The purpose of this research was to study the supply and demand issues that affect production and to assess the policy environment. In each country, research was carried out on the organization of production, market structures, socioeconomic information on the artisans themselves, supply and demand constraints, and government support programs. The overriding objective was to articulate a set of policy measures for each country that would improve the conditions of workers with a view to providing a more stable and secure future.

Previous Work

In Asia, socioeconomic studies on these industries are almost nonexistent. The exception is India, where there is much local case material on individual industries. Also, the overall policy environment has been studied to some degree. However, outside India, no published material was found aside from occasional mimeographed case studies. No one had taken the artisan sector and studied it in a holistic fashion. In short, the studies presented in this volume are the first of their kind for Nepal, Sri Lanka, Malaysia, Thailand, Indonesia, and the Philippines.

There are two reasons why so little work of this type has been carried out. Researchers, especially those who are well trained, are reluctant to engage in field studies where the units for analysis are widely scattered and often isolated. This is especially true of economists whose input is essential. Second, the existing data base in each country is extremely poor. This has led to a feeling of some despair in those who are interested, for example, in employment and trade earnings. This book will hopefully go some distance toward addressing these problems.

The Data Base

As stated, national data bases on employment and trade are poor. They are weakest concerning employment, where conjectures have to be made about both full- and part-time work. National census surveys always underestimate labour, where women work from the home and where children are involved, both characteristics of this industry. Trade data are better because exports have a high profile and the activity itself is amenable to quantification. However, trade data are often not sufficiently disaggregated. Furthermore, because standard classifications do not exist, different record keeping systems yield different results. In short, policy is not informed by the facts.

Issues in Data Collection

The researchers in this project had to confront a number of problems. Perseverance and hard work overcame most of these. The following will be of interest to those who might replicate this activity in the future.

- Where producers were also farmers, as was the case in Thailand, research interviews could only be done at night.

- In Nepal, because of the caste system, enumerators had to be selected on the basis of their caste. Newar students were used to interview Newar producers. However, this had the advantage of overcoming local language problems.

- In isolated areas, such as the mountains of Nepal, keeping warm and securing access to drinking water presented difficulties. Researchers often had to walk for a week to reach and return from field sites.

- In Sri Lanka, because the studied villages had previously been exploited by various groups, this project was seen by the villagers as a way to advance their own ends, especially for financial gain. As a result, in-depth interviews were used rather than structured questionnaires. Ultimately, it was important to identify both the researchers and the project itself with the needs of the village and the industry.

- In the Philippines, the names and addresses of factory workers had to be obtained outside the factory gates. Owners would not allow workers to be interviewed during working hours.

- In the Malaysian states of Sabah and Sarawak, both with large tribal populations, researchers found it necessary to go through two different levels of translation.

Overview of Policy Issues

The policy issues that were studied are both complex and fascinating. In many cases they reflect the problems of developing societies as they evolve through different stages of growth with all of the attendant trade-offs. Often, there are no easy answers. The main questions and issues that emerged were:

- Is it possible to balance production between exports and domestic use? The data from this project show rapid increases in exports, but a decline in domestic consumption. What are the consequences of this situation for employment and can small producers be protected from job losses through subcontracting arrangements with urban exporters? If not, what are the alternative employment opportunities?

- To what extent is it advisable to commercialize production, given the fact that an artisan's own creativity has always been considered indispensable? The evidence shows that large-scale structural change is taking place within this industry as a result of exports.

- What production arrangements best protect workers and provide for their welfare? Are producers better off in factories, or does this leave them more susceptible to exploitation than household-based workers where there is strong dependence on middlemen?

- What are the compromises between increasing output through the use of new technologies in factories and the subsequent unemployment that hits small producers hardest? By increasing output, a wider range of low-cost goods becomes available to the population in general, but widespread unemployment also results.

There has been very little debate on these questions within Asia. One aim of this project was to address these issues and bring them to the attention of policymakers. We have now seen this happen in some of the participating countries. However, a wider net needs to be cast, not only in Asia, but also we suspect in Africa and Latin America, where artisans face similar problems.

Regional Comparisons and Trends

This chapter highlights the main findings from the seven country studies presented in this publication. Analysis is done on a regional basis. It draws on primary field data contained in unpublished reports by the contributors (see bibliography for titles). Occasionally, other work will also be referred to for purposes of comparison.

Contributions to National and Local Development

National Employment Levels

Despite limitations in data. it is estimated that four million people work full-time on craft production, with another million occupied on a part-time basis. If figures were included for other major craft producing countries, such as China, South Korea, Hong Kong, and Taiwan, full-time employment would be over 20 million. The Ministry of Light Industries in China estimates that 10 million people are employed full-time, although its definition of a craft is broad (Anon. 1985).

Table 1. Estimates of national craft employment in the surveyed countries.

Country	Full-time	Part-time	Total
India	2 176 740	433 260	2 610 000
Nepal	597 781	617 219	1 215 000
Philippines	700 000	n.a.	700 000
Sri Lanka	139 334	37 486	176 820
Malaysia	44 468	78 032	122 500
Thailand	18 954	51 246	70 200

Sources: Figures for the total number of craft workers were obtained from: "1984 Report on Handicrafts" published by the All India Handicrafts Board; "1982 Industrial Sector Study Plan" by the Kathmandu Industrial Services Centre in Nepal; 1979 records of the Philippine Chamber of Handicraft Industries; "1980–81 Labor Force and Socioeconomic Survey" carried out by Sri Lanka's Department of Census and Statistics; "1980 Population and Housing Census," Malaysia; and "1981 Study Report on the Handicraft Industry" by Thailand's National Socio-Economic Development Board.

Employment figures (Table 1) for the surveyed countries would be even larger if accurate measuring techniques were used. At present, employment is underestimated in national surveys, as a result of the way census questions are formulated. Questionnaires do not deal with input from women working at home who are not household heads, from unpaid family members, or from schoolchildren, even though these groups form a sizable portion of the workforce.

Figures for part-time workers were obtained by applying the proportions reported in each of the country reports to the total number of workers (Table 1). There are two exceptions: in the Philippines, where these proportions are unavailable and in India, where proportions were taken from All India Handicraft Board surveys. For Malaysia, Sri Lanka, and the Philippines, full-time workers are defined as those working at least 6 hours per day; in Nepal, at least 22 days per month; and in Thailand, full-time workers are those who derive their primary income from the sale of craft products.

Although figures are generally not available on the sectoral composition of non-farm employment, craft production is clearly one of the key components. Additional research, however, is required to pinpoint the actual proportion of craft labour in nonfarm employment. Statistics presented later in this chapter show that for most artisan families, craft income often accounts for a sizable percentage of total household income.

These employment figures are extremely important in the context of land-scarce economies such as exist in south and Southeast Asia. In Nepal, for example, only 16% of the total land surface is cultivated; this leads to high land to person ratios, particularly in the hills and mountains where 60% of the population lives (Islam and Shrestha 1986). The cultivated area per person in the rural areas is 0.195 ha. In 1982, it was estimated that one hectare in the hills would need 298 person-days per year to be productive, 45% more than the actual figure. In Indonesia, the fifth most densely populated country in the world, 1.1 million new jobs are required each year in nonagricultural activities to keep wages rising with national income estimates (6% a year) and to prevent worsening income distribution. On the island of Java, where most Indonesians live, rice agriculture is the dominant activity, but provides employment to families owning one hectare or less for only 5–10% of the year. Many families operating rice land must find employment during the rest of the year in nonagricultural activities (Budiono et al. 1982).

7

Although national craft employment figures are not large in terms of the total workforce, this employment is critical within the local context. Craft income as a percentage of total household income shows this. Furthermore, craft units are widely dispersed throughout the country, often in remote regions where development programs do not exist.

Employment trends can be analyzed only in India where time-series data are available. In India, the number of new jobs created by craft industries during 1961–81 was almost as large as the number created by the private and public sectors combined. During this period, employment in the artisan sector rose from 1 to 3.5 million.

With the growing importance of exports, it is also clear that employment is shifting from rural to urban areas. In Indian jewelry, for example, where total employment increased by over 256% during 1961–81, employment in rural areas dropped from 64 to 44%. Similar trends were detected in almost all other Indian products except bamboo.

Where data are available, it appears that women may be losing ground. In India, in many of the high growth products, new jobs have been dominated by men. In jewelry production, for example, 98% of the work is now done by men; in the carpet industry the figure is 92%. Research must be undertaken in other countries to determine whether this loss is equally significant.

Foreign Exchange Earnings

Research shows high export levels for all countries. In India during 1978–79, trade earnings from crafts were greater than the total of all foreign aid disbursements (ILO 1983). Craft exports grew at a much higher rate during benchmark years (Table 2) than did overall trade.

A sizable portion of the total export earnings of India and Nepal is in crafts (Table 2). However, for the remaining countries, craft exports as a percentage of total trade are negligible.

Despite large increases in craft exports, Asian countries have not been able to diversify either their products or their markets. Most countries sell roughly 50% of

Table 2. Trends in trade.

Country	Average annual increase (%) in exports during benchmark years[a]		Craft exports as % of total exports[b]
	Craft exports	Total exports	
India	30.4	17.3	16.0
Nepal	31.2	5.2	13.2
Philippines	13.8	−12.3	2.3
Sri Lanka	64.8	13.5	0.7
Malaysia	26.2	15.4	0.3
Thailand	38.3	21.5	0.1

Sources: India, Director-General of Commercial Intelligence and Statistics; Nepal, Trade Promotion Centre's Overseas Trade Statistics; Philippines, Central Bank of the Philippines; Sri Lanka, Sri Lanka Custom's External Trade Statistics; Malaysia, Department of Statistics, Ministry of Trade; and Thailand, Thai Handicraft Promotion Division.
[a] Benchmark years are: India, 1972–83; Nepal, 1974–83; Philippines, 1974–83; Sri Lanka, 1980–83; Malaysia, 1970–83; and Thailand, 1970–82.
[b] Latest available figures.

Table 3. Annual income of producers in relation to national per capita income and receipts from agriculture.

	Malaysia		Nepal		Philippines		Sri Lanka		Thailand	
Per capita income (USD/year)[a]	1996	(1984)	145	(1984)	603	(1984)	340	(1984)	646	(1984)
Rural household income (USD/year)[b]	1817	(1985)	445	(1972)	1374	(1983)	505	(1979)	873	(1979)
Household poverty line (USD/year)[c]	1469		280	(1976)	818	(1983)	286		582	(1979)
Survey data on average household income of artisan families (1984) (USD/year)										
All sources	1989 (N = 457)		868		825 (N = 634)		1181 (N = 203)		1055 (N = 590)	
Agriculture	n.a.		511 (N = 257)		363 (N = 216)		n.a.		435 (N = 472)	
Craft production	828 (N = 457)		357 (N = 437)		285 (N = 634)		980 (N = 203)		386 (N = 590)	

[a] Source: *1986 Asia Yearbook*, published by the Far Eastern Economic Review.
[b] Sources: Nepal 1983, Sri Lanka 1964, IBRD 1980, World Bank 1985.
[c] Sources: Khan and Lee 1983, Asian Development Bank 1984, World Bank 1985.
[d] Includes earnings of all family members engaged in craft production, except for Philippines where only the artisan-respondent is tabulated. N may be less than the actual sample of producers because of missing data for some respondents.

their products to only one or two markets. In Nepal, carpets make up 94% of all exports. The situation is similar in other countries, although not quite as critical. This calls for immediate intervention by government and international agencies to open new markets abroad and diversify product lines.

Local Level Employment and Incomes

The income of craft households is above the poverty line and the national average in all countries except the Philippines (Table 3). This unexpected finding is due, partly, to artisan families' ability to combine agricultural, craft, and other nonfarm income sources. Also, families who make products for the tourist and export markets and rely on these goods for their sole source of income are generally responding to strong demand.

In countries such as India and the Philippines, incomes are lower. In India, the returns to labour are extremely low, due to a vast surplus of labour (not necessarily skilled) and the inability to organize for self-improvement. Because of this, high export earnings have not been shared equitably with the artisan. In the Philippines, a dependence on high-cost, imported raw materials, exemptions from minimum wages, and low agricultural returns are the main factors keeping craft incomes low.

Contributions to total household income are also important where craft production is clearly undertaken as a secondary source of employment. For example, in Thailand, where wicker workers are primarily rural farmers, craft sales represent 35% of total household income. This also holds true for other workers, such as Thai weavers and mat producers in the Philippines. These figures are consistent with other studies on nonfarm employment in Asia, which indicate that nonagricultural earnings may represent up to 60% of total huseold income in rural areas.

The export and tourist sectors provide significantly higher incomes than local markets in each of the surveyed countries. Brass in Sri Lanka, wood carving in Thailand, silver in Malaysia, and rattan in the Philippines all bring in significantly higher incomes than competing utilitarian products (Table 4).

The way in which an industry is organized has consequences for income levels. It was found that in Thailand, Malaysia, and the Philippines, factory workers drew substantially higher incomes than subcontractors or self-employed entrepreneurs working from the home.

Contrary to the prevailing notion, craft production is often a primary, not a secondary, occupation. A good example comes from the batik industry in Indonesia. This sector has traditionally been seen as providing secondary work, supplementing agricultural incomes and done in workers' leisure time. However, research shows that 95.8% of the batik workers in Java and 87.5% in Madura are employed for more than 5 hours a day and, furthermore, that 87.5% of this sample is engaged for more than 15 days per month.

Field surveys, especially from India, show that the wage intensity of different products, even within the same craft, varies enormously. For some, the cost of raw materials is high and wages are insignificant. In some Philippine craft industries, such as embroidery, materials may account for up to 94% of the total cost. For others, the opposite is the case. However, there is no deliberate attempt to promote products that maximize gains for the artisan.

10

Table 4. Annual income for workers according to product type.

	Sample size	Average income (USD)			Craft income as % of total
		Crafts	Other[a]	Total	
Malaysia					
Silver	53	1910	294	2204	86
Weaving	167	803	1416	2219	36
Plaiting	237	602	1176	1778	33
Philippines[b]					
Mats	152	122	291	414	29
Embroidery	146	194	694	888	21
Handweaving	87	346	502	848	40
Rattan	149	593	574	1167	50
Sri Lanka					
Brass	112	1272	249	1521	83
Pottery	91	619	144	764	81
Thailand					
Wicker	205	359	639	998	35
Woodcarving	160	536	539	1075	49
Weaving	225	305	789	1094	27

[a] Data on income from other sources are available only for Sri Lanka and the Philippines. For Thailand and Malaysia, they were derived by subtracting reported craft income from reported total income.

[b] In the Philippines, craft income refers only to the producer-respondent's income from crafts; craft income earned by other household members was included in "Other" income.

Conditions of Workers

The economic advantages of craft industries notwithstanding, it is widely recognized that as with other labour intensive industries, the attractiveness of establishing such firms is due largely to the availability of low-cost labour. Because the economic viability of the industry rests heavily on this factor, it is in the interest of entrepreneurs to hold wages down. Also, the oversupply of labour, which allows for easy replacement of workers at cheaper rates, leaves workers open to exploitation. Therefore, an assessment of the economic significance of crafts should be based not only on an analysis of employment and trade earnings, but also on an analysis of the welfare of these workers and the social and economic impact of employment on households.

Wages

As seen in Table 5, returns to labour are extremely low. For wool producers in Nepal and mat weavers and embroiderers in the Philippines, returns are less than USD 1 per day. In fact, researchers did not locate a single craft industry where the majority of workers were in the occupation primarily because of high income. For example, from the 205 cotton and wool workers interviewed in Nepal, only 12 stated that they were working as a result of attractive incomes. In the metal and wood industries in Nepal, only 10 among 155 interviewees cited high incomes. In Indonesia, from among 96 batik workers, none said that high income was the reason for his or her involvement.

Given the low wages, the survey found that workers are in the trade due to their own limited skill base, lack of occupational mobility, and ignorance of alternative employment opportunities.

Table 5. Returns to labour and duration of employment.

Country and product	Sample size	Average daily wage (USD)	Duration of employment (months/year)
Nepal			
Cotton	187	1.34	6.8
Wool	100	0.90	8.6
Metal	73	2.21	11.0
Wood	100	1.95	10.5
Philippines			
Mats	168	0.36	11.1
Embroidery	150	0.48	11.9
Handloom	97	1.10	11.4
Rattan	150	1.75	11.9
Sri Lanka			
Brass	105	5.58	12.0
Pottery	84	2.60	12.0
Thailand			
Wicker	205	1.79	10.8
Woodcarving	160	2.33	10.9
Weaving	225	1.00	10.4

Note: Malaysian rates could not be calculated because number of days worked per month was not known.

In Thailand and the Philippines where there are statutory minimum wage guidelines, all workers receive less than stipulated. In some urban industries, such as rattan in the Philippines, wage rates do, however, come close to the minimum level.

Research shows that it may be counterproductive for employers to keep wages low to improve the viability of their firms. When workers are denied a fair return, the result is often industrial inefficiency, low productivity, and poor morale, leading, in turn, to higher costs. Furthermore, the prevailing notion that higher wages are a threat to business viability was not borne out by the data, which show that rapid escalations in raw material costs are more significant.

Employment Stability

Employment is generally on a full- rather than part-time basis, especially for the production of export items, and periods of unemployment are fewer than might be expected (Table 5). This contradicts the prevailing notion that craft production is a part-time activity undertaken during leisure hours.

Despite this, there is unemployment, which varies with the market as well as the mode of production. The duration of employment has decreased with the adoption of labour-saving technologies. In Indonesia's batik industry, for example, handmade goods now compete with factory products. Large textile producers commonly flood the market with cheap batik imitations and engage in price fixing.

Due to fluctuations in the tourist and export markets, factories do not maintain a permanent or regular pool of workers, but contract or expand their work force in response to market demand. This is possible because of high unemployment rates and the high incidence of poverty in local households.

12

For some products, instability arises as a result of workers having to acquire specialized skills. For example, the training period required for making *halus* batik can be up to 10 years. These skills are not easily transferable and research shows that workers are unprepared to look for other employment when they are idle. Because the majority of workers see unemployment as their only alternative, they are willing to accept low returns. The inability to transfer craft skills into other types of employment is a common problem in all countries.

Women

Where direct comparisons can be made between wages of women and men, evidence shows that women are paid less for doing the same type of work. In the batik industry, women earn only 41% as much as their male co-workers for similar activities. In Java, 30% of the female respondents (compared with only 4% of the men) were single household heads with an average of three dependents. At the time of this research in 1985, a family of four, consuming 40 kg of rice, 8 L of oil, and 4 kg of sugar a month, spent INR 40 520 (14 Indian rupees (INR) = 1 United States dollar (USD) in 1988) on only these few staples. Monthly incomes for women in batik were only INR 17 175. The corresponding monthly pay for men was INR 41 167. Despite unequal rates of pay, women in all product lines contribute on average 28% of total household income.

Over time, there may be fewer employment opportunities for women than men. In India during 1961–81, men took two-thirds of the new jobs in rural areas where production took place outside the home. Except for bamboo, this trend is the same for other products in India. In other countries such as Thailand and Malaysia, women appear to remain dominant in industries that have traditionally employed females. However, we do not know the extent to which new jobs are being created in these fields.

The use of female labour in some of the industries studied is clearly inefficient. In the Philippines, for example, almost 40% of the subcontracted female embroiderers and handloom operators had either high school or college education. However, it should be pointed out that this situation does not exist in the other surveyed countries.

Occupational Hazards

In each country, it is clear that artisans rarely receive assistance against occupational hazards even though many of these industries are not safe. In Nepal, for example, among 73 metal artisans interviewed, only 4 received assistance, despite the fact that they inhaled metallic particles for long periods of time.

An excellent case study is the batik industry in Indonesia. Although seemingly safe, complications arise from the use of synthetic chemicals. Producers have begun to use caustic soda to extract dyes from plants and vegetables. These chemicals are sold in concentrated powder form and mixing is done without any protection for the lungs. Workers rarely use gloves or boots. Factories lack proper drainage facilities and in rural areas leftover synthetics and rinses are released directly into neighbouring streams. In factories, discarded liquid may sit in abandoned tubs in areas where workers cook, wash their dishes, or live.

Social Services

The availability of social services is linked to the scale and mode of production. There is no evidence in any of the countries that small, independent rural producers are able to provide medical or other benefits for their families.

Producers who do receive benefits are invariably part of a larger system of production. As the scale of manufacturing increases, so do the benefits. In the Philippines, for example, where rattan producers work in both large and small units, those who are employed by large firms may receive extensive benefits such as social and medical insurance, a thirteenth month pay, vacation and sick leave, company subsidized canteen rates, credit union facilities, emergency loan funds, rice subsidies, free clothing, separation pay, and retirement benefits.

Under subcontracting arrangements, benefits are sometimes provided as an incentive to increase production. In the Philippines, before periods of high demand, workers are often given free lunches, food subsidies, cash bonuses, etc., by entrepreneurs.

The Philippines is the one country in Asia where extensive benefits are found, yet it is also the only country where the government has deliberately exempted entrepreneurs from providing benefits. This action was taken as a result of strong lobbying by an urban-based pressure group.

Organizing for Collective Action

Organizing artisans to improve living and working conditions is important, but only one such case was found during this research. This was in the Kumbalgama region of Sri Lanka, where organized agitation by artisans led to a more secure source of raw materials, improved housing, and a training centre. In this case, artisans represented a large block of voters and had aligned themselves with a political party which was ultimately successful at the polls.

In some Asian countries, the political philosophy of the government itself is inherently biased against worker associations of any kind. In Indonesia, since the Communist revolt of 1965, it has been extremely difficult to organize workers into labour unions. Worker agitation is now associated with the banned Indonesian Communist Party.

Examples were found of entrepreneurs who deliberately fragmented the production process so that workers could not compete against them. In Java, factory batik workers are isolated from each other and the various steps in production are carried out in different parts of one building or in entirely separate locations. Few workers are allowed to master more than one skill. This is most common in rural subcontracting. The extreme division of labour has advantages for entrepreneurs, who keep competition at a minimum and exploit the availability of labour.

Supply Issues in Production

Problems relating to the supply of inputs vary enormously between countries, product lines, methods of manufacturing, and geographical location. Policy measures must be location and industry specific whenever possible.

Organization of Production

Despite high export levels, there is little evidence to suggest that large factories have taken hold, even in India. This is due to fear of unions and to legislation that does not allow manufacturers to lay off workers in slow periods. Entrepreneurs are unwilling to invest in factories that may remain idle during periods of weak demand; subcontracting is preferred. Labour legislation, except in the Philippines, also means that employers have to pay bonuses and contribute to welfare funds and insurance schemes.

The reluctance to invest in factories poses a major dilemma for policy. If one aim of policy is to promote welfare, the factory mode of production may be the best. As evidence from the Philippines, Thailand, and Sri Lanka suggests, factory employees are always paid higher wages and receive more benefits than those involved in subcontracting or household-based production. Balanced against this, however, is the fact that the cost of living in urban areas is high.

Except in Sri Lanka, subcontracting is extensively used by all entrepreneurs. However, research shows that there are major disagreements as to whether this type of production should be promoted. On one hand, data from the Philippines, Thailand, and Nepal outline various types of exploitation. However, producers from Malaysia and Sri Lanka have a different point of view. In Sri Lanka, artisans are anxious to organize production through the "putting-out" (subcontracting) system, but have been unable to do so as a result of inadequate links with firms in urban centres such as Kandy and Colombo. Subcontracting is therefore seen as a means of penetrating new markets and increasing production. However, because urban entrepreneurs do not have close links with village artisans, this has proved impossible. In situations like this, extension workers must provide the necessary linkages. In Malaysia, although small producers see disadvantages to subcontracting, such as a lack of control over the final price, supplies, distribution, and design, producers also feel that these drawbacks are more than compensated by the fact that all output is purchased by the entrepreneur and therefore salaries are secure.

Artisans entering a craft are rejecting the practice of working as part of a family unit within the household. In Sri Lanka, virtually all producers work within the home and contribute their time to the family. As the export market has not been fully exploited, there are few factories. Furthermore, the putting-out system has not yet taken hold. Research indicates, however, that this use of unpaid family labour is rejected by the younger generation and any attempt to develop crafts in which wage payments are not evident is unacceptable. A viable system must incorporate two elements: a cash wage and the social status acquired in going to work in a small factory or workshop. Research shows that this is the only production system in Sri Lanka that can realistically hope to attract and retain young crafts workers in the future.

There is general agreement among Asian policymakers that organizing artisans within cooperatives is a desirable objective. In some countries the entire mode of production is based on cooperatives. China's Ministry of Light Industries, for example, estimates that there are currently 61 000 cooperatives employing over 10 million craft workers. Burma and India have also invested large resources in cooperatives. The motivation in China and Burma is ideological, but there is a large body of literature to show that the vast majority of such ventures have been unsuccessful. The reasons for this include conflicts of interest between members, a lack of strong leadership or qualified management, and a continuing scarcity of capital.

15

The data collected from this project support this view. No examples of successful cooperatives were found at any of the study sites. Furthermore, national policies for developing cooperatives were found to be ineffective. The situation in Indonesia is typical. In this case, craft entrepreneurs have been encouraged by the government to organize to facilitate marketing and credit assistance. Virtually all of these endeavours have been unsuccessful and recently the Department of Cooperatives itself was forced to take over the National Union of Batik Producer Cooperatives because this cooperative had accumulated more than USD 3 million in debts. The government has not carried out feasibility studies to show whether there are cultural reasons why cooperatives have difficulty in Indonesia. Traditionally, craft enterprises are located within the household and are characterized by the belief that business is an individual responsibility. There has been a strong reluctance to share with others and to promote joint economic activities. As a result of this extreme type of individualism, cooperatives have been slow to flourish. In view of the fact that collective organizing is usually indispensable for the success of these small enterprises, it is urgent that government address this problem.

Training

Training remains overwhelmingly a family and village obligation (Table 6). As such, the costs of training, which are substantial, are still assumed by the family.

All governments spend heavily on training and have made it a central part of their development package. In Thailand, for example, over 20 000 government employees

Table 6. Mode of training by product.

Country and product	Sample size	Government programs (%)	Skills transfer within family (%)	Apprenticeship (%)	Self-taught (%)	Other (%)
Malaysia						
Silver	53	11.3	41.5	35.8		11.3
Weaving	167	13.8	74.8	11.4	n.a.	n.a.
Plaiting	237	46.8	41.4	11.8	n.a.	n.a.
Nepal						
Cotton	187	8.0	50.3	40.6	n.a.	n.a.
Wool	100	8.0	70.0	22.0	n.a.	n.a.
Metal	73	9.6	39.7	50.7	n.a.	n.a.
Wood	100	3.0	61.0	36.0	n.a.	n.a.
Philippines						
Mats	168	n.a.	45.8	2.4	47.6	4.2
Embroidery	150	n.a.	44.7	5.3	42.7	7.3
Handloom	97	n.a.	n.a.	40.2	14.4	45.4
Rattan	150	n.a.	12.7	50.7	31.3	5.3
Sri Lanka						
Brass	112	10.7	82.1	2.7	n.a.	4.5
Pottery	91	6.6	84.6	n.a.	8.8	n.a.
Thailand						
Wicker	205	n.a.	61.0	22.0	17.1	n.a.
Woodcarving	160	n.a.	54.4	27.5	18.1	n.a.
Weaving	225	0.8	76.0	8.9	14.2	n.a.

[a] n.a., not available.

are currently responsible for training in the cottage industry and craft sectors. Even in a less developed country like Nepal, over 13 000 artisans had been trained by the end of the Fifth Plan. Similar figures are available for other countries in south and Southeast Asia.

Despite the existence of these large training programs, very few of the producers interviewed had actually been exposed to them. The most extreme case was in Thailand, where among 725 artisans interviewed in Chiangmai and Lumpan provinces, both dominant centres of craft production in the country, only 1% had received support.

One of the most critical findings from these country reports was that the appropriate target groups are not necessarily receiving assistance. In Nepal, for example, training was heavily oriented toward cotton and wool producers, although research shows that wood and metal artisans were in greater need of assistance.

Training programs have not been related to the demand for products. To cite one example, the government of Sri Lanka established a master artisan training scheme for brass in the Embekke region. However, the fact that there was already an overabundance of brass artisans in the region had not been taken into account and, predictably, the dropout rate from this program was high. It would also appear that the methodologies for relating training to market demand are not well known; this is an area where technical assistance could play a useful role.

Another fundamental weakness in training programs is that artisans are taught a very narrow range of skills. This has greatly reduced their job mobility and left them exposed to periods of unemployment.

Surprisingly, despite the heavy investment in training, there is no evidence of any government having carried out an evaluation of these programs. In particular, evaluations have not been conducted to find out how many trainees have actually been able to use the skills and start a business. Research is also required into what skills students need to relearn over time, what gaps exist in training, and the usefulness of different training approaches.

In general, however, it is agreed that the skills transferred within the school system, whether within a classroom environment or outside, do not impart the talent required to produce high quality goods, especially of the standard necessary for export. This type of training is best undertaken through the apprenticeship system. However, government subsidies will be required given the high cost.

Finally, a fundamental flaw in existing programs is the emphasis on simply transferring a skill. In short, there is insufficient integration with other key activities. In Nepal, for example, although thousands of artisans have been trained, only 30% have been able to secure loans. The overall training package has not shown artisans how to secure credit and raw materials, or market their products.

Availability of Skilled Labour

There is clear evidence to suggest that the pool of skilled labour in many countries is quickly disappearing. In Malaysia, for example, one of the most disconcerting findings of this study was the aging of the workforce. The majority of artisans are now over the age of 40 and the sector is not attracting a younger generation. Although one reason for this is that school is compulsory for children, a more

17

disturbing note is the fact that parents do not wish to see their children enter the trade because of the lack of economic incentives and poor future prospects (Table 7).

In Sri Lanka, the pool of labour is also drying up, although partially for different reasons. In this case, although craft incomes are higher than those in agriculture, and even the civil service, young people refuse to take part in household work that does not pay a wage. Furthermore, the issue of social status is extremely important and has been a major contributing factor in the refusal of young people to join this sector.

In India, where the export trade is large, gains in exports over a very short period of time have strained the traditional system of skill transfer, which functioned well when demand was constant. However, it has not been able to respond in recent years to large increases in exports, especially those which occurred during 1971–81. As a result, skill levels have been lowered and there is a definite possibility that the country's large stock of excellent skills may disappear over time.

The situation is not as bleak in the Philippines, Thailand, or Nepal, but policy-makers would do well to note the trends. Thailand is fortunate in that the social stigma that is sometimes attached to craft work is not widely evident, perhaps as a result of the strong promotional effort put into this sector by the Royal Family. In Nepal, one of the world's poorest countries, poverty is so pervasive that any form of employment is readily accepted.

The Link to Agriculture

There is almost no literature on the link between craft production and agriculture, even though farming has a direct impact on production. In farm families where income from agriculture is low, income from crafts is indispensable. Research among agriculturalists in Thailand shows that wicker provides 32% of household income and cotton 35%.

Craft income is a good cushion for fluctuations in agricultural earnings. As farm income is highly seasonal, families typically experience several months of deficit followed by periods of cash surplus. Most farmers have difficulty in coordinating income with expenditure and resort to borrowing from money lenders at high interest rates. This feast-or-famine syndrome is substantially alleviated by income from non-farm sources such as crafts.

However, farming can also lead to severe shortages of craft labour. In Thailand, it was found that large proportions of workers left craft work for agricultural employment whenever this was necessary: 75% in weaving, 74% in wood, and 66% in bamboo. As a result, entrepreneurs who depend on such rural labour find it almost impossible to meet demand, especially during key periods of tourist activity and business expansion is all but impossible. Land preparation, transplanting, harvesting, and threshing constantly interrupt an entrepreneur's plans for production and expansion.

In Sri Lanka, artisans are leaving for a variety of reasons, among which agriculture plays a role. The government provides a guaranteed market for agricultural commodities and farmers therefore have a sense of security that is absent in the artisan. Artisans perceive that their main asset, skill, is not increasing over time at the same rate as the value of land. Land will always have a guaranteed return and will increase in value. This largely explains why Sri Lankan artisans who draw income from both sources plough savings back into land accumulation instead of crafts.

18

Research in Malaysia and Indonesia shows how agricultural policy itself can have a direct impact on craft earnings. In Malaysia, the government has pursued a policy of rural development that has focused on agriculture. There has been the implicit assumption that attempts to upgrade agriculture and the rural economy in general will also benefit small rural producers in cottage industries. However, because the supply and demand requirements of craft producers are different from those in agriculture, this assumption has not proven correct.

Government price policies for commodities such as rice can have a serious impact on the demand for craft products. In Indonesia, the price for rice is strictly controlled by the government and in 1985 was set at USD 0.25 per kilogram. In contrast, a piece of hand-drawn batik of average size costs a minimum of USD 4.50. That is, a farmer must sell almost 20 kg of rice to purchase one piece of batik. Given the fact that a farmer must also spend money on schooling, medical emergencies, etc., a piece of cloth made by a neighbouring rural household is beyond his means.

Raw Material Supplies

With the exception of a few utilitarian products made from freely available local materials, the regular supply of raw materials is a fundamental constraint to craft production. Supplies are irregular and costs are rising quickly. Furthermore, government programs have not been of assistance.

The majority of craft workers surveyed in this project are totally dependent on imported materials. One reason for this may be that the artisans who were surveyed are also producing for the tourist and export markets. However, it is precisely these sectors that are showing the fastest growth rates and providing most of the new jobs. Of 16 industries surveyed in 5 countries, 10 are dependent on imports.

In the Philippine textile industry, raw materials (yarn and thread) are all imported. In 1975, the cost of these materials represented 20% of the total value of the products. This figure rose to 57% for small firms in 1978, and in the same year to a staggering 94% for large firms. Such rapid increases in thread and yarn prices from abroad have made it difficult to determine the final selling price of a product. Because orders are taken several months before delivery, the price originally agreed upon is often no longer profitable. Furthermore, despite the devaluation of the peso, which should have provided an added advantage to exporters, the high domestic rate of inflation continues to erode gains. Naturally, when raw materials represent such a large portion of the final price, wages are reduced and the worker suffers.

Strangely, there is also evidence that imports are used even when the same materials could be produced locally. For example, the soil in the Philippines and Indonesia is suitable for growing cotton and has historically been used for this purpose. Despite this, cotton is still imported.

The high cost of materials and irregular supplies both act as a brake to business expansion. In the Thai teak industry, 38% of the wood entrepreneurs surveyed said that, due to scarcities, they will not expand production. Similar replies were received for other industries. Many small producers are resorting to illegal purchases on the black market. Examples of these were found in Thai teak as well as in rattan and embroidery in the Philippines.

There are numerous distortions in government policies, leading to competition for scarce resources between large and small entrepreneurs. In the carpet industry in

Table 7. Willingness of parents to allow children to continue in their trade.

	Sri Lanka		Thailand				Philippines		
	Brass (N = 112)	Pottery (N = 91)	Wicker (N = 205)	Wood-carving (N = 160)	Weaving (N = 225)	Mats (N = 168)	Embroidery (N = 150)	Hand-weaving (N = 97)	Rattan (N = 150)
Will artisans allow children to continue in their trade?[a]									
Yes	31	35	93	62	109	139	16	65	77
No	81	56	112	98	116	29	134	32	73
No answer	—	—	—	—	—	—	—	—	—
Why not?									
Income is insufficient	18	5	27	52	44	5	66	2	3
Labour is exacting	19	9	1	—	4	2	41	6	29
Work is for women only	—	—	—	—	—	—	—	—	—
Children should continue studies to have a better life	19	9	22	17	31	6	14	20	26
Children should decide for themselves	16	19	62	25	37	7	—	—	15
Other	9	14	—	—	—	—	—	—	—
No answer	—	—	—	4	—	4	—	1	—

[a] In the Philippines, the question asked was whether the artisans "will encourage their children to take on the craft."

India, for example, small producers making handmade carpets compete for the same supplies as large factories. When this occurs, the factories are certain to win. The consequences are an inevitable increase in price and a loss of trade and employment for the small producer. Second, preference is almost always given to firms producing for export, as against firms making products for local consumption. Again, this partly reflects the bias in favour of large firms that are active in the export trade. In the Philippines, for example, it was found that small producers have virtually no legal access to rattan, because almost the entire supply is going to exporters. Third, there is also a bias in favour of urban entrepreneurs. The Timber Cooperation of Nepal provides 80% of the wood to the country's wood manufacturers, but only one entrepreneur who received assistance from this source could be located outside of Kathmandu and Pokhara.

Three conclusions regarding government policy emerge. The most obvious one is the need for government regulation of pricing, especially where prices are not commensurate with rising material costs. In such cases, labour costs are reduced. However, mechanisms are not in place to monitor prices. Second, policies are irrelevant unless appropriate delivery mechanisms exist. In Malaysia, for example, the government has been concerned about the cost of materials and has established a scheme to provide supplies at controlled prices. This scheme was put in place some years ago, but nearly 73% of the 455 survey respondents had not heard of the program. Third, government monopolies would be more responsive if supply was also open to the private sector. In Nepal, the Cottage Industry's Handicraft Emporium is a public agency and has a monopoly on most raw materials. However, as a monopoly, it has no special incentive to regularize supplies or to meet demand adequately. Furthermore, demand projections for different sections of the country are not carried out systematically. In sharp contrast, the Wool Trading Company, another public company, has been able to regularize the supply of wool in a short period of time. In the wool industry, there are many private agencies involved in the import and distribution process, thus ensuring competition.

Technology

With the exception of brass and pottery in Sri Lanka and wood products in all countries, there is little evidence that power-driven machinery is used (Table 8). Reasons for not using available technology include: expense; concern that skills would be gradually lost; and belief that craft workers are more comfortable with traditional methods, that handmade products are more durable, and that mechanization will displace workers or result in loss of craft image with ultimate decline in markets. Users of technology, however, cite improved quality, increased production, lower costs, and lower prices as their rationale.

In Nepal, among 22 entrepreneurs interviewed, 12 indicated that they would not upgrade their technology, because the novelty of their products would be reduced resulting in a loss of markets. A similar pattern emerged in Malaysia among handloom entrepreneurs. In the Philippine embroidery industry, machines are seen as incapable of producing the elaborate stitching currently done by hand. It is believed that machine technology would be detrimental to the region's popularity in the market as a centre for hand embroidery, a reputation that at present allows producers to ask for higher prices. Entrepreneurs also say that they do not know how to gauge the appropriateness of some technologies, as they have no basis for comparison.

Table 8. Extent of technology use by country and product.

Country and product	Entrepreneurs			Producers		
	Surveyed	Using technology	%	Surveyed	Using technology	%
Malaysia						
Silver	22	0	—	53	5	9
Weaving	27	2	7	167	23	13
Plaiting	7	1	14	237	56	23
Nepal						
Cotton	110	21	19			
Wool	55	0	—			
Metal	50	12	24			
Wood	50	42	84			
Philippines						
Mats	15	0	—	168	0	—
Embroidery	15	2	13	150	0	—
Handweaving	7	4	57	97	0	—
Rattan	10	10	100	150	54	36
Sri Lanka						
Brass	31	31	100	112	107	95
Pottery	24	24	100	91	91	100
Thailand						
Wicker	20	4	20			
Woodcarving	30	17	56			
Weaving	20	1	5			

Note: In Nepal, technology refers to power or semi-automated looms for cotton and wool weaving and electric tools or machines for metal and wood work. In Thailand, it refers to power-driven tools for wicker and wood. Technology in the Philippines covers electric tools for rattan, sewing machines, and warping boards for embroidery and handlooms. In Sri Lanka, technology means unspecified machines or tools, and in Malaysia, "modern equipment."

There is evidence that policy could play a more active role in providing information. In many countries, entrepreneurs have not upgraded their technology, simply because they are not aware of the alternatives. Only 6 of 55 cotton and wool entrepreneurs in Nepal were aware of improvements in loom technology that could increase their output.

Among larger export-oriented industries, such as teak in Thailand and rattan in the Philippines, the use of technology is more widespread and involves a more complex set of factors. In Thailand, teak entrepreneurs are in keen competition with Taiwanese manufacturers, who are able to upgrade their technology more quickly, giving them an advantage in price. In the Philippines, the technology is so highly developed that it is now considered a trade secret and entrepreneurs will not provide information about their machinery. It should be noted, however, that even in this more mechanized industry, production is still labour intensive. Machines are used to prepare parts and for framing, with subsequent operations done by hand with the aid of special tools. It seems unlikely that the actual construction of rattan furniture will ever be completely mechanized. As one entrepreneur observed, the assembly process cannot be totally mechanized, as the "human touch will be lost." The situation is similar in Thailand where teak factories use large numbers of workers for carving the final products.

Despite the reluctance of some entrepreneurs to use power-driven machinery, the production of these crafts involves extreme drudgery and long hours; the need to improve conditions through suitable mechanization is obvious. Working conditions are very poor in many cases. There is no doubt that policy must play a more active role in improving conditions by making both information and technology available. However, research shows an almost total absence of government effort. In India, for example, among 72 craft workers interviewed in five fields, it was found that changes in design and techniques had been brought about only through their own innovation. Where government intervention was noticed, it was characterized by inadequate planning. Numerous examples are available. In the Sri Lankan study, an evaluation of one technology centre with millions of rupees of equipment shows that much of it had been used less than one hour per month, and some not at all, since its installation.

Finally, a word should be said about labour displacement. As rattan production in the Philippines and the teak industry in Thailand show, technology does not necessarily displace a great deal of labour. However, concern about unemployment is justified. In Java, for example, the introduction of new production technologies for batik imitations increased output by a factor of 2.35 and worker productivity 17.8 times, but at the same time the industry lost 20 000 jobs. Such losses always affect low-income workers most, while improved productivity usually benefits larger entrepreneurs.

Capital and Credit

The majority of producers, if they obtain credit, do so from noninstitutional sources, where interest rates are often three or four times higher than those charged by government institutions.

The main problem in expanding rural credit schemes lies within the banks themselves. The report from Nepal is typical: branch managers have little latitude where innovation is concerned and commercial banks have not been able to develop sufficient in-house expertise to accelerate loans or manage them properly. The main focus of their operations is short-term commercial credit. Furthermore, cumbersome bureaucratic procedures and high collateral requirements make the effective cost of loans far higher than the nominal interest rate. From among 155 cotton and wool entrepreneurs, 83 went to moneylenders to avoid the complicated lending procedures, 25 had insufficient collateral, and 42 were not licensed.

In India and Indonesia, lack of land may be the key constraint. In Indonesia, land is essential as collateral, but 51% of the artisans surveyed in rural Java and Madura are without land. The data from India are equally revealing. In 1971–72, the All India Debt and Investment Survey showed that for rural households with an artisan head, 99% were landless, compared with 36% of the population at large (Gordon and Levitsky 1979).

It should also be recognized, however, that even if banks were models of efficiency, subsidies would still be required for craft industries. A World Bank study in 1978, on transaction costs of lending by two Philippine institutions, shows that administrative costs for a given value of lending were eight times higher for small enterprises than for large firms and that default risks were twice as great. As a result, profit margins for banks involved in lending to small enterprises were not enough to cover the costs (India 1972). Research is therefore needed to see how such costs can be reduced, focusing on case studies of rural banking, such as those in Bangladesh, which have been highly successful with even the poorest rural producers.

Given the problems with the formal banking system, it is clear that informal credit plays a critical role in the production and expansion of artisan enterprises. Research also shows that noninstitutional credit has prevented many indigenous crafts from disappearing. Quick access to credit, regardless of the source, is especially important for purchasing raw materials. Among cotton and wool producers in Nepal, for example, although fixed expenditures are low, operating capital for raw materials is 25 times greater than fixed capital.

Artisans in Indonesia and Malaysia face serious problems due to the Islamic prohibition on interest. Rural orthodox Muslims will rarely pay interest and as a result do not have sufficient capital to expand. Profits are not sufficiently high to allow investment from personal savings.

Product Development and Design

Product development and design may be adversely affected by the way in which an industry is organized. In subcontracting, for example, entrepreneurs are rarely artisans, and workers themselves seldom innovate, so design suffers.

Although good design is imperative for the export market, research in India indicates that both the private and public sectors are almost totally inactive. In Sanjay Kathuria's (1988) study of Indian exports, among 49 exporters interviewed none was involved in design and development work. The only other industries in Asia that employ full-time staff for product development were rattan in the Philippines (due to size and dependence on exports) and the large batik enterprises in Indonesia.

Extension Workers

There are mixed results regarding the effectiveness of extension agents. In Malaysia, the experience has generally been useful, as the government has a well established network of training, production, and marketing centres that receive good support from the head office in Kuala Lumpur. There are incentives for office managers who run sound training programs, frequent staff exchanges, and considerable dialogue between extension workers and head office.

Reports from Indonesia are less optimistic. In 1974, the government established a major program to assist the craft sector through its industrial extension services for small industries. This program is well established throughout the country and provides training for entrepreneurs, improved technologies, purchasing of raw materials, and marketing assistance. The cornerstone of this program is the extension agents, located in villages and working with local entrepreneurs. Our research shows, however, problems in their effectiveness. Their low level of skill and lack of applied knowledge of small industrial development has lowered their credibility in the view of local entrepreneurs. Agents also too often lack the support of their superiors. They are employed on fixed, 2-year contracts and, therefore, have legitimate concerns about job security. All of these factors have led to poor motivation and frequent absenteeism.

In Sri Lanka, there is a problem in terms of implementing national policy for small enterprise development, including crafts, at the local level through these workers. National policy seeks to promote small enterprises to alleviate unemployment, but agents have no interest in small industries and believe that rural development hinges on agriculture and large-scale industrial development. As a result, national policy is not implemented and small entrepreneurs receive little support.

Finally, a typical problem throughout the region is that most extension agents are male, although the majority of workers are often female. This affects the quality of training, because, on one hand, the degree of formality appropriate to interaction between unrelated men and women impedes the process of hands-on learning necessary for crafts and, on the other hand, distrust of male outsiders makes local men reluctant to let their wives and daughters participate in training programs.

Export, Tourist, and Local Demand

Exports

Exports were found to be the key growth sector. Craft exports are increasing four times faster than overall trade. Given this promise, policy must address the constraints in the industry that will tarnish this growth.

All countries studied are heavily dependent on one or two nations for the majority of their sales and a country's exports comprise only a few products. There is clearly a need for both market and product diversification. Field reports suggest that the government must take the lead role. In Malaysia, for example, entrepreneurs indicated that they would be willing to penetrate new markets overseas only if government assistance was available.

Although the issue is seldom discussed, crafts are vulnerable to the same type of international trade retaliation as any other commodity. A vivid example of this is Philippine rattan, which was banned for export in its raw unprocessed form in 1977. This ban responded to the need to conserve supplies as well as to increase foreign exchange through higher value-added products. In retaliation, the United States, which is the Philippines' main source of demand, removed rattan furniture from its Generalized System of Preference. The furniture, which formerly had been shipped duty free, was suddenly subject to a 16% import tax. The Philippine government subsequently lifted its ban on rattan in March 1982, in exchange for a waiver of U.S. tariff policies.

Although a great deal of discussion takes place on regional cooperation, most countries in Asia compete against each other for the same markets, both locally and overseas. Thailand, for example, used to be a major supplier of wicker to the United States, but now only supplies 1% of U.S. imports, compared with 25% from China. Competition is also severe in carpets and in wood and metal crafts.

The importance of keeping shipping costs in line with competitors is discussed in the Indian case study on exports (Kathuria 1988). Partly as a result of high transport costs, India has allowed China to overtake it in the U.S. market. Furthermore, despite a favourable unit value, India's freight incidence is more than twice that of its most significant competitors, Korea and Taiwan, whether viewed in terms of value or quantity.

Governments will assist in a tangible way when demand is proven. Carpet making in Nepal provides a good example. Over the past decade, this industry has flourished and now accounts for 94% of all craft exports; craft sales account for 30% of total exports. Given this demand, the government has established a Wool Trading Company to assist in the regular supply of wool from Tibet and New Zealand.

Furthermore, the Cottage Industries Export Development Corporation has hired foreign consultants to provide information on competition and design. It has also opened an office in New York to advertise, increase international contact with importers, and collect information on product demand. This strong pull for one product has had spin-offs which will benefit numerous other products.

Despite such successes, however, much more could be done. In Nepal, researchers found examples of excellent pieces of legislation that could promote exports, but that have not been acted upon. In 1983, the government devised a nine-point export promotion program, so that banks could maintain a separate system for exports and extend pre-export credit. Unfortunately, this has not been implemented. Another piece of legislation, the Industrial Enterprises Act of 1981, sought to stimulate Nepali exports through the establishment of "export promotion areas." Important financial incentives were offered to companies locating in these export zones, such as 100% tax holiday for 10 years and a 50% rebate on income tax for the first 5 years. Despite these incentives, no zones have been established.

Finally, as discussed earlier, supply problems remain a serious hindrance. During 1980–83, Sri Lanka exported wood products to 52 countries that were stable and secure buyers. However, during the same period, the country lost export orders from 26 other nations, because it was unable to deliver quality goods on time.

Tourism

The tourist market accounts for only a small portion of total production. In India during 1970–71, exports totaled USD 104 million, while sales to tourists amounted to USD 8 million (Hone and Jain 1972). The data from Malaysia show an even more dismal picture. In this case, the average tourist spent only USD 2 on the three surveyed products combined.

The conclusion which can be drawn from the Malaysian experience is that there is a need to target products to the appropriate market. In Malaysia's case, the vast majority of tourists are from neighbouring countries and spend little money on crafts. Marketing should concentrate on Australian, European, American, and Japanese visitors, who spend more per capita on luxury items.

Utilitarian Products

Utilitarian products have traditionally been the mainstay of the crafts industry, but the situation has now changed significantly. In each country, factory products compete directly with handmade goods. To survive, entrepreneurs will have to expand into tourist and export sectors. This is already happening in the mat industry in the Philippines where producers facing extinction have branched into exports and in 1975 sold USD 12 million overseas.

Research also shows, however, that to capitalize on new markets, some centralization in production and marketing is indispensable; these functions are currently dispersed in different rural households. Centralization would allow for greater control over quality, which is now left to outside agents to monitor.

Another opportunity for growth, also found in the Philippines, is a "market encounter" where rural producers and urban buyers are brought together. Many buyers are surprised to see the range and quality of products that exist. Demand may not be saturated, but may simply need to be primed by such government-initiated programs.

The future of utilitarian products is related to the degree to which the local infrastructure is developed. Nepal has only 3 km of road per 100 km² and a difficult terrain. Factory imports move slowly and expensively into the inner areas. Thailand, in contrast, has 18 km of road per 100 km² and a relatively well integrated economy. Here, rural producers making utilitarian goods are in danger of losing their livelihood and must expand to survive.

Government Policies and Support Programs

All countries surveyed in this project, except for the Philippines, have moved their economies forward in recent years. However, in each case this has been the result of high prices for agricultural products and natural resources. These prices have now plunged and there is no evidence that the high returns of the past will come back. Asian policymakers are looking for substitute exports or ways to increase the value of traditional ones.

The craft sector brings in much more than is spent on it. In India, for example, from 1960 to 1984, craft exports earned INR 90 billion in foreign exchange, but the sector received only INR 1.4 billion from the government in return (1951–85). However, if the sector is to maximize its potential, it will require not only more liberal financing, but also an improved set of policies. This is especially the case for export-oriented industries, which need more complex support programs.

Recent Interest

In a number of countries, we find a more active recent interest in the craft sector. This is the result of higher-than-expected unemployment figures, worsening debt-service ratios and the inability of large-scale, capital-intensive industries to fulfill the original expectations of planners. India, on the other hand, has historically both promoted and protected its craft industries, although many would argue the effectiveness of various programs. In Sri Lanka in 1982, parliament undertook a full-scale debate about the rationale for supporting artisan industries when it passed the National Crafts Council and Allied Institutions Act No. 35. In Nepal, artisans were given top priority within the cottage industry sector during the Sixth Plan, 1980–85. In Thailand, one of the foremost objectives of the new Sixth Plan is the creation of jobs through rural industrialization, of which craft production is a major component.

Absence of Long-Range Planning

What has more aptly characterized planning over the past 20 years is the absence of a long-range component. There are three reasons for this. First, with the exception of India, no country has been able to decide what group of industries make up the artisan sector. As a result, there is no official definition to guide decision-making. The consequences of this can be seen in Nepal where "cottage industries" constitute one category of industry and support policies generally apply across the board. However, this classification includes industries as divergent as distilleries, detergent manufacturers, and artisans. In the Philippines, there are too many definitions. Different classifications for artisan industries are used by the Central Bank, the National

Association of Cottage Industries, and the Philippine Chamber of Handicraft Industries. In Malaysia, customs officials use their own intuition about what constitutes craft on a case-by-case basis with, not surprisingly, vastly inconsistent results.

A second reason for a lack of long-range planning is, in some countries, the inability of planners to agree on rationale for investing in the sector. The best example comes from Sri Lanka, where transcripts are available from 1982 parliamentary debates on the National Crafts Councils and Allied Institutions Act. Policymakers were seriously divided. Some felt that the sector was a repository of culture and tradition, with its roots firmly anchored in the past and little to offer in the present. Others identified artisans as constituting one of the most disadvantaged segments of society and believed that investment was therefore required to raise living standards. Other officials emphasized the potential for trade and employment generation. There was no consensus on the ultimate rationale for investing scarce resources.

Third, and most important, is the fact that data are unavailable — both quantitative data and conceptual and analytical research on problems within the industry. More is known in Sri Lanka about 18th century birds than about the country's artisans. In the absence of this information, it is not surprising that officials find it difficult to articulate long-range strategies. Fundamental data, such as numbers of people employed, are not available in any country except India. In the Philippines, for example, the National Association of Cottage Industries estimates that the country has 43 000 artisans, but the Chamber of Handicraft Industries believes the figure to be 726 000. Trade data are more readily available, but lacking in detail.

What are the immediate consequences of this situation? Too often money is not wisely spent. Planners tend to put large sums of money into training. Statistics are then marshalled to show how many thousands of workers have been "trained." To most officials, this appears to be a fairly straightforward type of development program and something worth supporting. However, particular industries, in which training and exposure to new technologies are needed, are not receiving it and money is wasted on those who do not require it. Research is rarely carried out to determine whether there is a market for the products that these new workers will manufacture and evaluations are almost never done to see how many people are actually able to use the new skills to make a living.

Although large sums are spent on training, very little is allocated to product development, new market penetration, or finding means to improve wages. Manufacturing remains largely oriented toward mass production, although exports require quality control. The emphasis on labour intensity has meant that insufficient attention has been paid to improving wages. Admittedly, these problems are all more difficult to resolve than those inherent in training, but they are also more important.

Bias in Industrial Policies

Industrial policies favour large industries, despite the fact that over 90% of the industrial labour force in each country, with the exception of Malaysia, is employed in the small-scale sector. These policies work against small artisans in a number of ways: important financial incentives, including tax holidays and depreciation allowances, are not available; and support agencies supplying raw materials and credit tend to focus their efforts on urban areas. Small producers can expect little help, except for training and an occasional visit from an extension worker.

On a more positive note, the bias toward large firms works in favour of those who export — an important trend, given research data showing that exports must be emphasized if small craft-producing firms are to survive. Export promotion agencies are already in place, but these now must be upgraded and brought into contact with a wider set of markets. These agencies must shoulder some of the responsibility for the concentration of craft exports in very few markets.

Multiplicity of Agencies

We found, somewhat unexpectedly, that in each country there were too many, rather than too few, support agencies. It was assumed that, given low financial allocations, there would also be a lack of institutional support. However, some countries such as Malaysia have over 12 support institutions. It was beyond the ability of this project to evaluate thoroughly the effectiveness of each of these, but the following conclusions can be made.

There is a waste of funds and a duplication of effort. In Malaysia, for example, there are six agencies involved in marketing and also six cooperatives. Second, the delivery of services has been adversely affected. Data from the Philippines and Malaysia show that field operations are not coordinated between institutions. Ironically, the very problems these agencies were established to resolve still remain.

Conflicts in Policy

In some countries, especially those with large textile industries, there have been serious conflicts between policies designed to promote production and those dealing with employment. In Indonesia, for example, recent measures to stimulate the output of batik cloth for the country's large domestic population, as well as for export, have been highly successful, due to the use of factory scales of production. At the same time, the government has emphasized job creation schemes that have been unsuccessful in cities such as Solo (central Java), due to the widespread closure of small batik enterprises that are unable to compete with the factories. Before the arrival of these factories, Solo had over 3000 small workshops making batik cloth, many employing up to 15 workers. There was great creativity in design and colour, and traditional motifs flourished. Now 12 workshops remain. The situation is similar in Yogjakarta, also in Java, where from among 648 batik entrepreneurs registered with the government in 1958, only 34 (5%) are still active. Again the reason is factory competition. Small textile producers in Sri Lanka and India have met the same fate, and the Indian situation is well documented. In Sri Lanka, competition did not come from large domestic factories, but rather from imports encouraged by liberal economic policies in the early 1980s. As a result, the entire handloom industry collapsed. After this, the government shifted course, but found that it was almost impossible to rebuild the production base once it had been destroyed.

There is little point in attacking factories or legislating against them. After all, they produce cloth at a cheap price and for low-income families. The role of policy, therefore, should be to segregate markets so that a certain portion is reserved for small producers. At the very least, alternative employment opportunities should be provided. At the present time, it does not appear as though these issues are even debated.

Promotional Policies

Despite scarce resources, governments will invest in promotional programs if a good return is guaranteed. In Nepal, for example, which is the poorest of the countries surveyed, the strong demand for carpets led to the establishment of an office in New York for promoting exports and the hiring of foreign consultants. These are expensive undertakings, but show a confidence, backed up by data, that justifie the expenditures on exports.

The overall environment for promotion is more favourable in countries that view artisans as a national resource. Thailand is the best example of this. Here, artisans do not suffer from a low social standing and the industry is not viewed as residual. No doubt, the promotional work of the Royal Family on behalf of artisans is partly responsible for this. The country also has a large number of well- managed foundations that work in this sector. At the other end of the scale, data from Sri Lanka show that artisans suffer from low prestige; although they may have incomes higher than farmers or even civil servants, they are leaving their trade partly as a result of social pressure. This may account for the less than agressive promotional campaigns put on by national agencies in Sri Lanka.

Finally, most governments have realized that the private sector is better placed to market products. Not only do private entrepreneurs have better contacts with rural producers, but they also have more extensive relationships overseas. In Thailand, the government has recently increased its dialogue with private associations, such as the Thai Chamber of Commerce, and has also gone into joint ventures with the private sector. One such venture is between the Department of Industrial Promotion and a private firm that has invested in and is now managing Naraipan, an established network of retail outlets previously run by the government. In Nepal, the government has formed links with private entrepreneurs to increase exports through its Cottage Industries Export Development Project.

Future Prospects

Evidence shows that exports hold the key to the future. The demand for utilitarian goods has declined in most countries, and sales to tourists are still negligible, although this is also a market which will increase. It is in the export sector that we see large gains in each country. Craft exports have risen dramatically and, in each case, much faster than overall trade.

If the future lies in exports, however, this will have major consequences in terms of existing support policies. An export-oriented industry would tend to move production to the cities, a result that goes against the national policies of all governments, and requires greater amounts of capital and technology than are presently available. Training programs will have to be improved and upgraded. Furthermore, unless the gains in trade are shared more equitably with producers, the current stock of skills will disappear. At present, returns to labour are so low that the lack of a respectable wage is an enormous disincentive. However, an export-oriented industry would have a number of key advantages: benefits are more extensive; wages are higher; and, perhaps most important, a future built on exports holds more promise.

While exports are growing rapidly, the workforce is aging. In Malaysia, the average artisan is now 40 years old and in Sri Lanka, 41. In the Philippines, Thailand,

and Nepal the figures are 34, 32, and 27, respectively. These data are based on information from 2300 respondents and are representative of what is happening throughout the region.

The work force is aging because in most cases parents are not allowing, or encouraging, children to enter the trade (Table 7). Although existing producers plan to remain, new talent is not available. The reasons for this vary, but are generally related to low income, lack of security, and low social status. Higher incomes and greater prestige accrue in the export sector, which requires factory modes of production and therefore pays a monetary wage. However, if artisans refuse to enter the trade, this sector will soon decline as well. It is not clear whether policymakers are aware of these facts, but quick action is needed.

Field studies show that in general the endowments, constraints, and prospects of each craft industry differ by country as well as regionally. Support policies should be industry and location specific as much as possible. Within a region and industry, planners are likely to find that the demand for locally consumed goods is decreasing and, in time, will probably disappear. Given the importance of the craft sector for creating employment and substantially improving household incomes, this loss is serious. To retain jobs, producers should be encouraged to shift production to the export and tourist sectors wherever this is feasible. In doing so, the government must play a key role so that the transition is orderly and rural-urban migration is reduced through appropriate subcontracting policies. Fortunately, most countries have a large number of development agencies to assist. However, in the most critical activity, penetrating new foreign markets, a wider set of actions is necessary. Here it is essential that international agencies with technical expertise, such as the International Trade Centre (Geneva), the Center for the Promotion of Imports from Developing Countries (Rotterdam), and Oxfam Trading International (Bicester), expand the important functions they are already performing. Bilateral donors may also be applied to more extensively and effectively than has been the case to date. Private sectors in both developing and so-called developed countries need more opportunities to come together to exchange information on product development, demand trends, technological innovations, and tariff policies. This is a difficult and expensive process and requires assistance from all of the institutions noted above, including national trade and investment agencies.

Nepal

This study of artisans in Nepal takes place among unusual contrasts. Centuries of Buddhist and Hindu culture, largely isolated from outside influences, have acted as rich sources of artistic inspiration, and yet, with a per capita income of only USD 160 per annum, Nepal is one of the world's three poorest countries. Artisans work for a living in the midst of enormous poverty and hardship. Because craft production is an important source of employment, and trade earnings now account for 13% of all exports, the economic environment is at least as important as the cultural. In Nepal, artisans are assisted by a poor national treasury and sell products to people with very low incomes — not a highly favourable environment. Yet field evidence shows that craft workers have done surprisingly well.

It is important that craft policy be well developed in Nepal, because artisans play an important role in alleviating unemployment, now endemic in the country. The economy is overwhelmingly agricultural, but the rugged terrain, erosion, and population growth have made farming increasingly difficult. Only 16% of the total land surface is cultivated. In 1977, the National Planning Commission stated that the rural labour force is underemployed for approximately 64% of the year (Nepal 1977). A recent study shows that in the hill and mountain areas, where 60% of the population lives, one cropped hectare must employ 298 person-days per year, but is actually absorbing 45% less (Islam and Shrestha 1986). Craft production, which is widely dispersed throughout the country and provides full- as well as part-time employment for agricultural families, is one important means of addressing this problem.

It was within this context that this research on Nepal's artisan communities was carried out. The objective was to look at the role of artisans in development, collect primary data so that their constraints could be more fully understood, and relate the information to ongoing government policies. Researchers were unable to locate any previous studies of the artisan sector that used more than a few villages for sampling. This earlier research was not nationally representative and focused on only a few products sold in limited markets. Furthermore, no one had attempted to analyze existing census and trade data. The present study combines national data with empirical evidence from household studies to spotlight an important part of the economy.

Research was carried out from July to December 1984. A total of 250 enterprises were studied, representing 779 artisans and entrepreneurs in both rural and urban settings. To capture the dynamics of different markets, cotton and wool were selected for studies representing utilitarian products; 291 artisans and 165 entrepreneurs in these fields were interviewed. In contrast, the metal and wood industries are geared toward tourist and export sales; in these crafts, 73 and 100 artisans and 50 and 100 entrepreneurs, respectively, were contacted.

Table 9. Artisan employment in various occupations by age group.

Product	Age group	Number of respondents	Main occupation					
			Agriculture		Craft		Other	
Cotton								
Kathmandu	6–14	8	(0)[a]	1	(0)	5	(4)	2	(2)
valley	15–60	82	(42)	50	(15)	28	(25)	4	(2)
	over 60	0		0		0		0	
Outside the	6–14	51	(31)	9	(5)	33	(26)	9	(0)
valley	15–60	418	(226)	137	(51)	175	(135)	106	(40)
	over 60	11	(5)	0		0		11	(5)
Wool	6–14	22	(17)	1	(0)	6	(4)	7	(6)
	15–60	214	(117)	52	(28)	137	(67)	25	(22)
	over 60	23	(16)	5	(3)	7	(3)	1	(0)
Metal	6–14	35	(11)	3	(0)	22	(9)	10	(2)
	15–60	175	(71)	22	(16)	115	(42)	38	(13)
	over 60	13	(6)	4	(2)	7	(3)	1	(1)
Wood	6–14	32	(8)	7	(3)	16	(4)	9	(1)
	15–60	242	(87)	80	(46)	104	(18)	58	(23)
	over 60	6	(3)	5	(3)	1	(0)	0	

[a] Figures in parentheses indicate number of female respondents.
Note: Number of respondents does not necessarily equal the number under "main occupations" as some respondents have other sources of income not listed here.

Contributions to National Economic Development

Employment

Table 9 shows artisan employment in various crafts by age group, and Table 10 lists national employment statistics for major categories of artisan products by region. Employment in crafts (175 702) as a percentage of total cottage industry employment (Table 11) is a relatively low 14%. However, it must be remembered that approximately 97% of all craft labour takes place in the hill and mountain regions where development assistance programs are weakest, and, therefore, the need for employment creation programs is greatest. The impact on employment from this sector is not so much the number of workers as the fact that it is highly diversified and operates in remote regions.

Foreign Exchange Earnings from Exports

The value of various craft exports, compared to total exports from 1974–75 to 1982–83, is given in Table 12. (Data for sales to tourists are not available.) Four interesting findings emerge. Foreign exchange earnings from crafts are a sizable 13.2% of all trade; it appears that the contribution of this industry to trade overshadows the employment factor. This is the opposite of what one might have expected to find in Nepal. Second, if one looks at earnings in 1980–81, when sales figures were at their highest and compares these with 1982–83 statistics, in every case but one (handweaving) earnings have decreased. In many cases the drop has been substantial. Third, gains in trade have been the result of fast increases in carpet sales, which now account for 94% of all craft exports. This is up from 22% in 1974–75. Fourth, the fact that 57% of all Nepali craft exports go to just one market, West Germany, is cause for concern.

Table 10. Estimated employment in selected craft industries by region.

Region	Cotton	Wool	Metal[a]	Wood[b]	Total Number	Total %
Mountains						
Households	9 532	7 843	50	—	17 425	16.1
Individuals	13 881	11 722	150	—	25 753	14.7
Hills						
Households	62 067	24 525	476	300	87 368	80.6
Individuals	103 384	40 303	1190	750	145 627	82.9
Tarai						
Households	3 541	—	—	—	3 541	3.3
Individuals	4 322	—	—	—	4 322	2.5
Total						
Households	75 140	32 368	526	300	108 334	100
Individuals	121 587	52 025	1340	750	175 702	100
Distribution						
by craft (%)	69.3	29.7	0.7	0.4	100	

[a] Brass and bronze only.
[b] Wood turners excluded.

Source: Compiled from population census reports, APROSC research studies, and industry-specific data from the Industrial Services Centre.

34

Table 11. Relative status of cottage industries in Nepal, 1977/78.

	All industry	Cottage and small industry	
		Number	% of all industry
Number of establishments	754 000	751 000	99.6
Employment	1 271 000	1 215 000	95.6
Production (NPR million)[a]	3288.1	713.0	21.7
Value-added (NPR million)	698.3	218.8	31.3
Investment (NPR million)	826.1	341.1	41.3

Source: Sixth Plan, Part 1, NPC Secretariat, Kathmandu.
[a] 17.6 Nepalese rupees (NPR) = 1 United States dollar (USD).

National Policies and Programs

Definitions

Fundamental to our understanding of the artisan sector in Nepal is the fact that an official definition of a craft does not yet exist. The development of this industry has suffered from the lack of definition and, consequently, lack of appropriate policies that respond to its needs. Since the First National Plan in 1956, crafts have been classified as a cottage industry. However, within the cottage industry sector there are also industries producing plastics, detergents, chemicals, drugs, and medicines, all having little in common with crafts. Nevertheless, many cottage industry policies apply uniformly to all these categories.

The Industrial Enterprises Act of 1981, which revised definitions for cottage industries, now considers these to be enterprises where investment in machinery, equipment, and tools does not exceed NPR 200 000 in value (in 1988, 22 Nepalese rupees (NPR) = 1 United States dollar (USD)), and where fixed assets do not exceed NPR 500 000 in rural areas and NPR 800 000 in urban areas. Cottage industries are therefore classified in terms of value and fixed assets and do not take into account either the markets in which they are sold or the products themselves. Definition of the craft sector and a streamlining of relevant policies are urgently required.

Industrialization and Cottage Industries in Nepal

As Table 11 shows, the number of cottage industries as a percentage of total industrial units is 99.6%. Employment as a percentage of total industrial employment is also dominant: out of an industrial labour force of 1.271 million, 1.215 million people are employed in this sector. However, cottage industries' share of total and industrial GDP is low and declining, from 33.7% of industrial earnings in 1974–75 to 29.2% in 1978–83 (Table 13). Because crafts are a cottage industry in Nepal, one can assume that this sector is also declining over time in terms of employment and output, carpets being an exception.

National Plans

Because a separate and easily identifiable set of policies for craft development does not exist, it is important to look at government programs for cottage industries. A shift can be seen in more recent years toward craft products within the cottage sector.

35

Table 12. Value of craft exports (NPR thousands) compared to total exports, 1974–83.

Commodities	1974/75	1975/76	1976/77	1977/78	1978/79	1979/80	1980/81	1981/82	1982/83
Wood and bamboo goods	230	467	616	896	979	1 197	1 959	702	1 579
Paper products	2 899	2 266	1 202	4 496	5 412	2 507	46 228	371	714
Handwoven cloth	142	20	—	141	241	67	38	48	40
Woollen goods	6 705	2 772	3 924	5 035	5 460	6 707	10 245	5 144	562
Carpets	7 853	9 276	27 906	23 944	45 819	55 367	65 590	83 929	137 702
Gurkha knives	53	76	84	108	47	135	160	18	97
Metal figures	17 508	12 743	20 559	17 813	20 782	18 763	28 083	6 308	3 634
Thankas				7 047	9 076	16 288	55 840	1 228	801
Filigree				7 166	6 268	5 901	11 763	3 473	836
Other crafts	—	—	—	2 251	5 421	2 020	4 467	1 236	828
Total	35 390	27 620	54 291	68 897	99 505	108 952	224 373	102 457	146 793
Total exports (NPR million)	889.6	1208.7	1189.0	1065.2	1303.6	1166.3	1612.7	1496.0	1112.7
Craft exports as % of total exports	4.0	2.3	4.6	6.5	7.6	9.3	13.9	6.8	13.2

Source: Trade Promotion Centre, Overseas Trade Statistics, various issues.

Table 13. Contribution of cottage industries to total and industrial GDP.

| Fiscal year[b] | Industry earnings (NPR million)[a] | | | GDP (NPR million) | Cottage industry share of | |
	Cottage	Other	Total		Industry (%)	GDP (%)
1974/75	224	440	664	16 571	33.7	1.4
1975/76	231	459	690	17 394	33.5	1.3
1976/77	237	499	736	17 280	32.2	1.4
1977/78	263	531	794	19 732	33.1	1.3
1978/79	289	559	848	22 215	34.1	1.3
1979/80	318	618	936	23 351	34.0	1.4
1980/81	337	712	1049	27 307	32.1	1.2
1981/82	369	820	1189	20 265	31.0	1.8
1982/83	399	969	1368	33 621	29.2	1.2
Annual compounded growth rate, 1975–83 (%)	7.5	10.4	9.5	9.2	−1.7	−1.9

Source: Central Bureau of Statistics, Kathmandu, Nepal.
[a] In 1988, 22 Nepalese rupees (NPR) = 1 United States dollar (USD).
[b] Fiscal year begins in mid-July.

During the first two national plans, 1956–65, there was very little emphasis on industrial development of any kind and no allocation for cottage industries. In the Second Plan, this sector received only NPR 10 million or 0.6% of total government allocations. Higher investments in the industrial sector were hardly possible, in view of the resources available and the institutional and administrative structures prevailing at that time. Furthermore, the government was occupied in expanding the transportation infrastructure and improving the land tenure system.

By the Sixth Plan, 1980–85, however, allocations for cottage industries had risen substantially. Funding had increased to NPR 500 million, or 11% of total national spending. Furthermore, craft products were now being recognized for their economic importance, and agencies were established for assistance. In fact, within the cottage sector, crafts were receiving priority treatment for reasons of employment.

By the end of the Sixth Plan, the following government agencies had been established to provide assistance to cottage industries, including crafts.

- Cottage Industries Development Board: training, technical, and consultancy services; design work; preparation of new craft products and distribution of these products to craft workers; provision of raw materials, credit, and marketing assistance to new entrepreneurs; and assistance to artisans in remote and backward regions.

- Department of Cottage and Village Industries: licensing and registration of new industries.

- Cottage Industries and Handicrafts Emporium: provision of raw materials and marketing assistance.

- Agricultural Development Bank of Nepal and the Nepal Rashtra Bank: credit.

- Cottage Industry Export Development Project, located within the Trade Promotion Center: export assistance.

Evidence from the Field

Census and trade data give us some idea of the role of artisans in national development. It is clear from the preceding tables and analysis that they are a significant factor in generating foreign exchange. Employment levels are not comparably high, but important in that they represent widely dispersed enterprises providing employment for low-income, agricultural, and other wage earners. However, a more complete picture emerges from studies aimed at the household level. The following analysis summarizes the situation with regard to the four major products studied by this research team.

Employment

Artisan households have a diversified income base. Of 1302 respondents, all of whom make crafts full or part time, 48% list craft production as their main source of income, but 30% cite agriculture and 21% other work as their primary source of employment. This ability to draw employment from more than one source is important in a country like Nepal where the rural labour force is underemployed for 64% of the year. Women are important contributors to household income; 46% of the surveyed artisans were female.

When entrepreneurs were questioned (Table 14), all but seven said that employment among their workers was either increasing or remaining constant. It is important to note that metal and wood are both export- and tourist-oriented products. In short, these households will have higher incomes than the average Nepali family because they have capitalized on numerous sources of employment, the women work, and many are employed in the growing export and tourist sectors.

Wages

Although cotton and wool workers are paid on a per piece basis through subcontracting arrangements, daily wage rates have been calculated for purposes of comparison. Weavers of cotton shawls, saris, *dhakas*, and other garments earn NPR 17.6–37.6, calculated on a daily (8-hour) basis. Workers in wool earn NPR 12.4–22.3 per day.

Table 14. Trends in full-time and seasonal employment reported by entrepreneurs.[a]

Location and craft	Full-time employment			Seasonal employment		
	C[b]	I	D	C	I	D
Kathmandu Valley						
Metal ($N = 29$)	22	7	0	19	6	4
Wood ($N = 50$)	35	12	3	38	12	0
Outside the valley						
Metal ($N = 21$)	17	4	0	17	4	0

[a] Each of the 50 metal and 50 wood entrepreneurs was asked to give two responses, one in relation to full-time employment and the other for part-time.

[b] C, constant; I, increased; D, decreased.

These are extremely low returns, amounting to less than USD 1 per day for approximately an 8-hour period. This reflects the nature of subcontracting, whereby the producer has no leverage over the entrepreneur, but is totally dependent on this agent for supplies of raw materials and for marketing. The producer is not in a position to bargain for higher wages.

The situation in metal and wood crafts is different, reflecting stronger markets. Returns are significantly greater for the more skilled workers. Unskilled wood workers earn NPR 22.0 to 22.5 per 8-hour day, while skilled artisans earn NPR 45.6–64.5 per day. Craft workers making decorative metal products earn NPR 27.5, 34.5, and 68.9 per day for wax work, casting, and carving, respectively; those making household utensils earn NPR 26.7, 38.22, and 64.2 for the same jobs. Wages in these industries compare favourably with the national per capita income level of USD 145 per annum.

Skills Transfer

Despite the heavy investments in training made by the government, very few artisans have, in fact, been trained through formal programs. This is especially surprising in the wood industry where workers are usually employed full time and where there is a strong demand for skills upgrading (Table 16). In fact, part-time female workers in cotton and wool report a higher exposure to formal training than wood artisans. It is therefore relevant to ask in which industries formal training programs have been taking place. Despite considerable government efforts, the appropriate target groups are not necessarily receiving assistance.

Occupational Hazards

Traditionally, little emphasis is given in any developing country to the employment conditions of artisans, and this is especially the case in low-income nations like Nepal. Most surveyed artisans reported health hazards related to their work, and only 20 (7%) of those reporting hazards received assistance from their employer (Table 15). In trades such as metal and woodworking, serious complications arise from inhaling metallic and wood particles over prolonged periods of time. Among the 118 metal and wood artisans experiencing difficulty, only 4 received assistance. In cotton and wool crafts, the nature of prevailing subcontracting arrangements leaves most of these workers with no assistance from entrepreneurs.

Table 15. Incidence of occupational health hazards among artisans.

	Artisans reporting hazards		Artisans reporting assistance from employer	
	Number	%	Number	%
Kathmandu Valley				
Cotton (N = 151)	91	60	12	13
Wool (N = 100)	72	72	2	3
Outside Kathmandu Valley				
Cotton (N = 36)	28	78	2	7
Metal (N = 73)	52	71	4	8
Wood (N = 100)	66	66	0	0
Total (N = 460)	309	67	20	7

Raw Material Supplies

Cotton and metal entrepreneurs are in the most precarious position in terms of a steady supply of raw materials, because these materials are all imported: cotton, brass, bronze, and lead come from India. Even wool is imported in sizable quantities from Tibet. Wood is the only commodity among the four industries studied that is not imported.

Three problems were identified. First, the greatest problem for cotton and wood entrepreneurs within the Kathmandu Valley is that of artificial shortages caused by private hoarding, and followed by an increase in price. Second, supply problems are also caused by increased demand, usually following the monsoon period, when agriculture is in a low cycle and craft production picks up again. Third, entrepreneurs in the rural areas outside Kathmandu and Pokhara are not receiving their fair share of supplies. The Timber Corporation of Nepal supplies 80% of all wood to private dealers, but not a single entrepreneur outside Kathmandu reported receiving assistance from this source.

Credit

The majority of entrepreneurs are dependent on noninstitutional sources of credit. Of 246 entrepreneurs surveyed, 83% did not have access to bank loans. The reasons they gave for this situation were: lending procedures are complicated, 63%; their production units were not registered, 20%; and they lack collateral, 17%. Given the higher interest rates charged by noninstitutional sources, these entrepreneurs have an average loan size which is much lower than those going to banks (NPR 3889, compared with NPR 14 967. Noninstitutional interest rates average 25%, as against 10% for bank loans. This is important, as entrepreneurs require large amounts of capital for stocking raw material supplies. In cotton and wool, for example, although fixed expenditures are low, operating capital for raw materials can be as much as 25 times the value of fixed capital. Bank loans are generally less available outside of the Kathmandu Valley.

Major Constraints to Growth

The absence of a steady supply of raw materials requires the government's attention; 38% of artisans surveyed and 80% of entrepreneurs cited this as a major

Table 16. Major constraints reported by artisans.

	Raw material supplies	Training	Credit	Wages	Markets
Kathmandu Valley					
Cotton ($N = 151$)	66 (44%)	47 (31%)	0	92 (61%)	23 (15%)
Wool ($N = 100$)	17 (17%)	39 (39%)	4 (4%)	76 (76%)	3 (3%)
Metal ($N = 73$)	28 (38%)	19 (26%)	0	36 (49%)	26 (36%)
Wood ($N = 100$)	43 (43%)	67 (67%)	0	85 (85%)	38 (38%)
Outside Kathmandu Valley					
Cotton ($N = 36$)	22 (61%)	21 (58%)	0	23 (64%)	21 (58%)
Total ($N = 460$)	176 (38%)	193 (42%)	4 (1%)	312 (68%)	111 (24%)

Note: Rows do not total 100% because more than one answer was given by some respondents.

constraint to their work (Tables 16 and 17). In addition, and consistent with previous findings, training for wood artisans is required. Credit is not a problem for artisans, but it is for entrepreneurs. Marketing assistance remains a need for both. These are all areas where government infrastructure is already in place to provide assistance.

Future Perceptions of the Trade

The majority of surveyed artisans in cotton, wool, metal, and wood plan to continue to earn a living through these occupations (Table 18). However, few (6%) cite income as the motivating factor. Instead, respondents are evenly divided between those stating that their skills are not transferable elsewhere (41%) and those reporting that alternative employment opportunities are unknown to them (48%). These results support previous findings that demand per se is not a constraint. Rather, insufficient income, especially in cotton and wool, is the primary factor.

Conclusions and Recommendations

The major effect of the artisan sector on employment is not its size, but the fact that it is widely dispersed throughout the country, including the most remote regions where few, if any, government employment programs have much hope for success.

Table 17. Major constraints reported by entrepreneurs.

	Raw material supplies	Training	Credit	Marketing	Technology
Kathmandu Valley					
Cotton ($N = 99$)	81 (82%)	9 (9%)	41 (41%)	60 (61%)	7 (7%)
Wool ($N = 11$)	7 (64%)	4 (36%)	3 (27%)	8 (73%)	0
Metal ($N = 50$)	37 (74%)	5 (10%)	35 (70%)	23 (46%)	10 (20%)
Wood ($N = 50$)	40 (80%)	4 (8%)	10 (20%)	35 (70%)	11 (22%)
Outside Kathmandu Valley					
Cotton ($N = 11$)	7 (64%)	3 (27%)	7 (64%)	4 (36%)	1 (9%)
Wool ($N = 44$)	41 (93%)	7 (16%)	15 (34%)	22 (50%)	3 (7%)
Total ($N = 265$)	213 (80%)	32 (12%)	111 (42%)	152 (57%)	32 (12%)

Note: Rows do not total 100% because more than one answer was given by some respondents.

Table 18. Primary reasons for artisans continuing in or leaving their trade.

	Kathmandu Valley		Outside Kathmandu Valley			
	Cotton	Wool	Cotton	Metal	Wood	All
Reasons for continuing ($N = 360$)						
Employment alternatives unknown (%)	43	32	47	48	66	48
Skills nontransferable (%)	43	57	32	42	26	41
Income attractive (%)	6	4	11	6	7	6
Other (%)	8	6	11	5	2	6
Reasons for leaving ($N = 100$)						
Income insufficient (%)	74	85	82	25	60	74
Demand poor (%)	6	12	6	62	20	14
Other (%)	19	3	12	13	20	12

Combining craft production with agriculture has resulted in substantially higher and more stable employment for artisans. Families that draw wealth from crafts as well as from agriculture have annual income levels which are three times higher than the national average.

Policy has emphasized labour intensity, but data show that wages for utilitarian goods are as low as USD 1 per day. It is, therefore, necessary to balance creation of employment with improved returns. Low wages, especially in the utilitarian goods studied, offer little incentive for artisans to remain in the trade. That people are doing so is simply a reflection of the fact that other employment is unavailable or their skills are not transferable. From a policy point of view, a more positive environment must be created through the use of carefully selected technologies, improved training programs, and marketing assistance.

Over time, there has generally been a consistent growth in demand from the export market, which now accounts for 13% of total trade earnings. In 1974–75, the comparable figure was only 4%. To solidify this performance, certain critical steps must be taken. With the exception of carpets, export earnings in every product category declined during 1980–83. The reasons for this must be investigated. Second, with the exception of woodwork, most craft production relies on imported materials. Not only does this decrease total exchange earnings, it also puts producers in a precarious position. The need for government intervention to ensure a stable supply is, therefore, evident. Third, the majority (over 90%) of trade earnings come from carpets, and the direction of trade for all craft products is too heavily dependent on one market, West Germany, which takes 57% of Nepal's craft exports. There is need for product and market diversification.

Formal training, as currently provided by the government is not required for the entire craft sector. Skill transfer for some products, such as cotton, is best left to the family. This also saves scarce national resources. However, there are two areas where policy could be improved. First, research is necessary to identify industries that could profit most from formal programs. Wood is one example of an industry that is not receiving sufficient attention. Responses from wood producers and entrepreneurs indicate that lack of training is a serious constraint to growth of their businesses. Second, training should be an integrated package, including more than a transfer of skills. It must also cover entrepreneurial development and management training, as well as programs for low-interest credit and marketing. At present, this type of integrated approach is missing. Artisans are currently trained to make a product and are then left to their own resources. In the present economic environment of Nepal, this is a questionable approach (Sharma and Upadhyay 1985).

Credit was not found to be a constraint in some industries — a fact that in itself has policy implications. However, when credit is required, it is often not extended, due to the government's own complicated lending procedures. These procedures have less to do with collateral requirements than with cumbersome bureaucratic regulations. Bank managers have little latitude in making decisions, and commercial banks have not developed sufficient in-house expertise to accelerate lending or to manage loans properly.

In the case of raw materials, government agencies are not supplying producers outside the towns. Furthermore, a regular and reliable flow of materials has not been achieved. It would be advantageous to remove the monopoly that the Cottage Industries Handicrafts Emporium has on some materials. As a monopoly, this agency has little incentive to meet demand on a regular basis or to carry out systematic demand projections.

A large number of government agencies have been established to provide assistance. This is a clear recognition of the important role played by craft industries. However, a master plan to assist the sector does not exist. As a result, these agencies are less than effective. There are too many organizations with overlapping functions and a conspicuous lack of coordination between them.

Some agencies have devised excellent programs for stimulating sales, but these have not been put into action. One example is the Nine Point Promotion Program to extend pre-export credit. Another is the Industrial Enterprises Act, which offers tax holidays and income tax rebates. Industries in wood and woolen goods could benefit from this legislation if it were acted upon.

It should be noted that the Government of Nepal is not unaware of some of these problems and has taken a step toward rectifying them through the Cottage and Small Industries Project, collectively funded by the World Bank and the United Nations Development Program. This program is concentrated in the Kathmandu Valley and the Gandaki Zone, which includes Pokhara, and provides assistance for both production and marketing. Two important export products, carpets and garments, have received particular attention. It is estimated that this USD 12 million program will create 10 000 new jobs, stimulate the national income by NPR 120 million per year, enhance traditional skills, assist local communities to become more self-reliant, and contribute significantly to foreign-exchange earnings. An evaluation of this program is not yet available, but it appears to be a step in the right direction. Nevertheless, it should be noted that even in this case crafts have not been diffentiated from other small industries in terms of development assistance.

Sri Lanka

As a small island economy with a limited population, Sri Lanka has not favoured heavy industry in its industrialization process. Resources have not been available for importing the requirements of large industries, such as technology and technical expertise, raw materials, and the necessary finances. With a serious unemployment problem, especially in rural areas, the government has looked to small industries to absorb much of this labour. The First Public Investment Program of 1979–83 stated that one of its objectives was "the promotion of small and medium-scale industries, particularly in the rural areas, where unemployment is the most severe" (ILO–ARTEP 1986, p. 1).

The magnitude of the unemployment problem can be seen in data on land ownership. Although the economy is overwhelmingly agricultural, available land declined from 1.8 ha per person in 1901 to 0.4 ha in 1979 (Marga Institute 1985). Although the small-industry sector has been viewed as offering one remedy to this problem, policies have differed. Before 1977, when the Bandaranaike government was in power, small industries were promoted to encourage import substitution. Since 1977, there has been a shift in emphasis to foreign exchange earnings. As the Public Investment Program of 1985 states: "The small and medium industry sector provides a reservoir of vast potential for accelerating export-led industrial development. These can be linked vertically as a supply base for large industries" (ILO–ARTEP 1986, p. 2).

It was within this context — a concern for employment and trade earnings — that this study of artisans in Sri Lanka was undertaken. Its main objective was to shed some light on the role of artisans in the country's development, particularly from a policy point of view. This study is the first of its kind in the country; only two previous papers exist on Sri Lanka's artisans, both unpublished and neither based on primary data (Lyanage 1978).

Research was carried out in 1984 among 203 brass and pottery producers, as well as 54 entrepreneurs, to capture the dynamics of the local markets. In addition, six case studies were done on export firms selling abroad. Because this project did not cover all the regions of the country, but was confined to locations within one day's drive of Colombo, it is not a national study. However, almost all the country's export firms are located in the Colombo region, and it is doubtful whether problems of rural craft workers in other locales differ considerably from those studied here.

In looking at national statistics on craft employment and trade, this project faced data restrictions that are characteristic of Sri Lanka's small-industry sector as a whole. A 1986 International Labour Organization report on small enterprises in Sri Lanka states:

> An immediate stumbling block facing any attempt at evaluating the small and rural industries sector of Sri Lanka is a lack of any systematic information on its size and structure. More frustrating is the fact that whatever scattered data exists is rather difficult to place together in a coherent picture. Due to the variety of ways in which small industries are defined by different agencies of the government . . . the plethora of definitions naturally leads to a welter of confusion and renders the task of data collection an extremely difficult one. (ILO–ARTEP 1986, pp. 3–4)

The present study confirms this point of view. No national-level data on craft employment exist, so estimates can only be made by looking at the number of firms. Trade data are more readily available, although they are imprecise.

Finally, researchers found that a definition of what constitutes a craft product has not yet been accepted by the government, although the issue has been vigorously debated in parliament in relation to the National Crafts Council and Allied Institutions Bill of July 1982, which established a number of government agencies to promote this sector. As a result, policymakers in Sri Lanka have varying views of the craft sector: as a repository of culture and tradition, rooted firmly in the past; as a disadvantaged segment of society whose living standards must be raised; or as a potential area for increasing rural incomes and employment. Some officials subscribe to all or at least two of these points of view. However, no explicit policy about the role of craft production in Sri Lanka's economic development has yet been established.

Craft Employment Within the Industrial Sector

Before we look at craft labour, three issues must be recognized. First, 97% of total industrial employment is in the small-scale sector, that is, 50 people or less per production unit. The only industries in the country in which more than 50 people per firm is common are the petroleum/coal and plastics sectors; even here, 88 and 85%, respectively, of producers are small scale. For all industries, 1983 Industrial Census statistics show that among the country's 104 866 manufacturing units, 103 846, or 99%, employ fewer than 50 people (ILO–ARTEP 1986, p. 5). The labour intensity of the country's industrial sector is clear. Second, time series data on employment are not available. One can arrive at only rough trends by piecing together data from different sources. Third, statistics are available showing the number of industrial units per product type, but not employment by product. These are serious limitations to analysis.

Although employment statistics are not available, the number of units for various artisan products is known and provides evidence on what is happening to employment (Table 19). Steep declines are apparent in the number of production units for all products except furniture. The magnitude of this drop should be cause for serious concern. The textile industry has been affected by economic liberalization policies which have allowed large-scale imports. Other categories such as pottery and rope have suffered from substitution of synthetics and cheap imports. Other declines no doubt have arisen as a result of inadequate production and marketing policies. Using a different set of data for 1983 only, Table 20 illustrates the sectoral composition of the craft industry in Sri Lanka. These data show the rural character of this sector and a high concentration of units in textiles, liberalization policies notwithstanding.

Foreign Exchange Earnings

Trade earnings from craft exports indicate cause for both concern and hope. Craft exports have risen faster than overall trade earnings, increasing from LKR 43 million in 1980 (in 1988, 32 Sri Lankan rupees (LKR) = 1 United States dollar (USD)) to

Table 19. Changes in the number of selected craft production units in Sri Lanka, 1971–83.

Craft product	Number of production units	
	1971[a]	1983[b]
Handwoven textiles	12 102	6 325
Wooden furniture	979	2 012
Jewelry	2 789	1 726
Pottery	2 959	1 697
Cane ware	1 664	907
Coir rope	13 140	807

Sources: Data for 1971 were taken from Sethuraman and Bangasser (1984); 1983 data are from Sri Lanka (1986).
[a]Firms employing less than 50 people in rural and urban areas, excluding Colombo.
[b]Units employing less than 5 people in rural and urban areas, excluding Colombo.

Table 20. Number of craft units for selected products, employing less than five people per unit, 1983.

Craft product	Number of production units		
	Urban	Rural	Total
Spinning, weaving, and textiles	183	6 142	6 325
Furniture	396	1 616	2 012
Wood and cork	151	1 662	1 813
Jewelry	339	1 387	1 726
Pottery and china	9	1 688	1 697
Carpets and rugs	44	1 561	1 605
Clay	39	1 536	1 575
Cane ware	76	831	907
Rope and twine	21	786	807
Total	1 258	17 209	18 467

Source: Sri Lanka (1986).

Table 21. Export value of various craft products, 1980–83.

Product	Export value ('000 LKR)[a]			
	1980	1981	1982	1983
Handcrafted wood products	19 537	277 779	31 452	39 460
Basket work, wicker work, articles of plaited material	3 784	1 167	14 137	1 475
Handloom products	2 412	6 829	3 256	8 175
Batiks, powerloom	29	16	105	281
Knotted carpets, rugs, tulle, tapestries, embroidery	1 998	3 752	6 239	1 305
Pottery	165	909	257	202
Jewelry, precious metals	12 709	5 717	20 236	41 380
Other articles of precious metals	554	0.5	0.8	8
Imitation jewelry	48	7	2 647	220
Copper and brass ware	434	849	4 993	30 668
Pipe and reed organs	4	15	0.5	0.1
Tortoise shell articles	64	75	5	0.2
Toys	2 577	3 390	6 341	58 906
Total of handicraft earnings	43 914	52 132	89 671	182 082
Total of all export earnings	17 273 185	19 917 663	21 124 140	25 182 699
Craft earnings as % of all export earnings	0.25%	0.26%	0.42%	0.72%

[a]In 1988, 32 Sri Lankan rupees (LKR) = 1 USD.

LKR 182 million in 1983 (Table 21), a notable achievement, considering the lack of government programs for promoting craft exports.[1] However, the level for 1983 is only 0.72% of total trade earnings and compares unfavourably with a more disadvantaged, land-locked country like Nepal, where craft earnings now account for 13% of total exports. The situation is further clouded by the results of field surveys, which were done in preparation for the six case studies on export firms. Researchers obtained a list of 116 licensed exporters from the Ministry of Trade. Only 26 of these firms could be

---

[1] There are two fiscal incentives in place to promote craft exports: the Export Finance Scheme, which makes short- and long-term credit available; and the Export Development Grants Scheme, which rewards exporters on the basis of their performance and encourages entrepreneurs to invest in product development and market penetration.

located and, among these, only 16 were exporting. Although Sri Lanka is covered by the GSP, 70% of the companies licensed to export in the late 1970s have shut down, some without filling a single order.

Many of the country's largest export products, such as wood, copper, brass, and toys, have lost markets that were once secure. These particular items have lost a large number of purchasers: 30 out of 49 countries have stopped buying toys; 26 of 52 no longer buy nontoy wooden products; 11 of 46 have discontinued brass and copper imports. One common explanation can be found in each of these cases: poor quality control. One government document that examined the loss of craft markets overseas states:

> The crippling constraint in the export of Sri Lanka handicrafts has been the inability to supply quality products on time. While it is absolutely necessary to investigate how and why such a large number of markets were lost, the obvious constraints, observed at the production end, have continued unheeded. High moisture content in wood, which with time causes splinting and shrinking, the rising cost of timber, scarcity of required varieties of timber . . . and the inadequacy of common facilities at least in relation to pre-crafting, are among the crippling constraints at the production end. (Sri Lanka 1983, p. 121)

On the loss of markets for toys, it concludes:

> The ineffective adherence to stipulations pertaining to toy safety and injury proof requirements, for example toxicity of crafting materials, splinter resistance of wood, ingestible character of the toys or its components, etc. has opted Sri Lanka out of the international toy market. (Sri Lanka 1983)

Evidence shows a seemingly contradictory picture of an export sector that grew by over 300% between 1980 and 1983, but lost major markets due to poor quality control. Various factors lie behind this contradiction. The market is being successfully exploited by a few new large firms, some of which employ hundreds of workers and can no longer be considered small-scale. These new firms, relying on improved technology and superior management, are partially responsible for the high growth of exports. On the other side, markets are being lost by the more traditional traders, who have not exercised sufficient quality control. It seems that the market is not being fully exploited by all traders and that there is ample room for growth, provided that domestic supply problems can be overcome.

Evidence from the Field

Questionnaires were administered in six villages, representing three pottery and three brass producing communities. These products are primarily for domestic use in Sri Lanka, although some goods are also sold to tourists. Craft occupations in these villages are caste-bound and generally represent the lower end of the scale. A total of 203 artisans (91 potters and 112 brass workers) and 54 entrepreneurs (24 in pottery and 30 in brass) were surveyed.

Employment and Income

Our survey of producers indicates a relatively high level of employment stability throughout the year, as well as fairly long working days. The majority of workers in both industries work 6–10 hours per day (68.2, 93.7, and 75.0% in the three brass producing villages and 98.2, 51.0, and 65.6% in the pottery making villages). Of the workers surveyed, about a third work 16–20 days per month and another third work 21 to 25 days per month. In addition, these artisans enjoy remarkably high income levels, well above the national rural average of LKR 600 per year (Table 22). This is surprising, considering that the producers in this study were low-caste artisans who make products for local consumption, where returns are generally lower.

Detailed interviews with craft workers, however, show a disturbing trend. Although craft incomes are higher than those in agriculture, and the standard of living for artisans is generally better, most artisans compare themselves unfavourably to agriculturalists. As a result, there has been a movement away from crafts. The explanation lies in a perception that their "capital" or skill will in time erode in value compared with the value of land. Furthermore, the government provides a guaranteed market for agricultural commodities. Farmers, therefore, have a sense of security not found in these artisan communities, where there are fears about the future demand for their products. This is an important area for policy to address.

The Organization of Production

Virtually all production takes place through the use of unpaid family labour (Table 23). This is typical of other crafts in the country, where production is also

Table 22. Distribution (%) of total income of artisan families in the six villages.

					Potters	
		Brass producers		Helambawa-		
Monthly income level (LKR)[a]	Pahala Beligalla ($N = 49$)	Embekke ($N = 36$)	Kalapura ($N = 32$)	tawana Sengal Oya ($N = 33$)	Kumbalgama ($N = 22$)	Molagoda ($N = 40$)
0–200	1.9	—	—	—	—	—
201–400	17.0	—	3.1	6.1	6.7	2.0
401–600[b]	13.2	3.9	—	39.4	6.7	3.9
601–800	22.6	15.7	6.3	18.2	3.3	3.9
801–1000	15.1	27.5	6.3	9.1	23.3	3.9
1001–1400	15.1	29.4	25.0	21.2	20.0	13.7
1401–1800	9.4	9.8	21.9	3.0	26.0	23.6
1801 and over	5.7	13.7	37.5	3.0	14.0	49.0

[a] In 1988, 32 Sri Lankan rupees (LKR) = 1 USD.
[b] National rural average is LKR 600; 45% of the total population is below this line.

Table 23. Organization of labour in the six villages.

	Unpaid family labour (%)	Wage labour		Contract at piece rate (%)
		Permanent (%)	Part time (%)	
Brass producers				
Pahala Beligalla ($N = 121$)	77.8	0.8	21.5	0
Embekke ($N = 49$)	73.5	2.0	12.2	12.2
Kalapura ($N = 94$)	76.6	4.1	2.4	16.9
Potters				
Helambawatawana				
Sengal Oya ($N = 60$)	93.4	0	0	6.6
Kumbalgama ($N = 52$)	94.2	0	5.9	0
Molagoda ($N = 102$)	96.0	0	1.0	3.0

located in the home. Because the export market has not been fully exploited, there are few factories. Furthermore, the putting-out system has not yet taken hold. Research indicates that using unpaid family labour is a key factor in the decision of young craft workers to leave this type of work. An attempt to develop crafts through the cottage industry system of production, in which the pooling of unpaid family labour is a key part, is not acceptable to this group. A more viable production system would be the development of small workshops using wage labour. A new system for crafts must incorporate two elements: a reliable wage and the social status of a "worker" going to a workshop or factory to do a job. Research shows that this is the only production system that can realistically attract and retain young craft workers in the future.

Credit

Most artisans have no debts at all or very small loans. Among the artisans surveyed, 67% owed LKR 1000 or less (52% of the loans were under LKR 500). Although some entrepreneurs had larger loans outstanding, 67% owed nothing at all.

There is little use of institutional credit except in the village of Kalapura where 42% of borrowing producers used banks. Interest rates are reported as "zero" in cases where a middleman extends loans interest free and buys the products back, although, it should be noted, at a reduced rate averaging 5%. Interest is, in fact, charged, but it is much lower than the rate of 60% and above undertaken by the majority of workers who borrow in Embekke and Kumbalgama.

Government Intervention

The government has been active in all these villages, and four cases of intervention are revealing. In Embekke, a training program using master artisans was undertaken for brass workers. An evaluation of this program indicates three problems. The scheme has not been carefully structured by the Department of Small Industries, nor have the norms for training been adequately set. The master artisans, representing an older generation, relate to their students on the basis of traditional norms that guided relationships between them and their apprentices in the past. These norms permitted teachers to expect various domestic and personal services from students during the training period. The master artisans of Embekke have attempted to relate to their apprentices on the basis of these traditional attitudes. The students, on the other hand, belong to a younger generation and have been exposed to different political, social, and cultural values that have made this type of service distasteful. As a result, the drop-out rate has been high. On the supply side, there are more brass workers than the market can absorb and, therefore, the need for additional training in brass is highly questionable. Finally, the level of skill that has been passed on to students has been low. For the most part, students have left their training period with poor skills and have been unable to produce products of a marketable quality.

On the other hand, in the village of Molagoda, the government's training centre for potters has had a positive influence. Demand for products from this centre has been good, and 30% of the sale price is returned to the producer. After training, most artisans have successfully opened their own businesses. The centre maintains its support by continuing to provide technical advice and by placing orders on a subcontracting basis. Partly as a result of this centre, fewer artisans are leaving their trade than in other villages.

Another example of successful intervention is in the village of Kalapura, where the government was instrumental in opening up new markets through its chain of Laksala stores. Laksala outlets were established in 1964 and remain the most important retail outlets in the country. They were started even before exports had become important and before the emergence of the middle class as a purchasing power. They were intended to provide an outlet for rural artisans and to stimulate demand for their products; these goals were successfully met through the 1960s and 1970s. Access to Laksala, via the Department of Small Industries and through personal links with officials, gave Kalapura artisans a clear advantage in marketing their products. They soon began to enjoy higher levels of income than craft workers in other villages. However, by 1981, Laksala faced stiff competition from the private sector, and purchases declined.

Finally, another example from Kalapura is the Common Facilities Centre, built to provide the benefits of modern technology to local artisans. The centre was equipped with a wide range of machinery: an electric welding plant, spinning lathe, carving machine, sheet-folding machine, sheet cutters, metal disk cutters, sheet formers, wire-drawing machine, electric hand drills, lathe, and polishing machine. Total government investment in this workshop was LKR 2.5 million. However, an evaluation of the project reported:

> Its record of use to craftsmen proved . . . a dismal failure. The use of all machines in this centre put together has averaged less than one hour per day, and some of the machines have averaged less than one hour of use per month. Some of the equipment has not been used since its installation. Researchers found that this centre was more a symbol of state concern for craftsmen, which was commendable, than a facility which responded to the actual needs of the beneficiaries. A concept of a common facilities centre is a good one provided that it is equipped with machinery which is actually needed by craftsmen, but cannot reach artisans' homes due to the financial costs involved. (Linyanage n.d.)

Raw Material Supplies

Research shows that a regular supply of materials is not available either to rural producers or to exporters. In pottery making, the depletion of white clay has led to the substitution of other substances with the result that products often crack. Metal workers find that brass, copper, silver, and polishing liquid are all imported. Supplies are not predictable and prices are unstable.

On the export side, two case studies are illuminating and point out the critical nature of the problem. A Colombo exporter had established strong links with a West German company regarding design, technology, and marketing for certain wood products. A large order was received for the German market. Instructions specified that no artificial colouring was to be used, but that the wood was to be cut and shaped in such a way that, when the pieces were closely fitted together, their natural shade and grain provided the desired design. In his attempts to fill this order, the exporter found that private dealers did have a few varieties of wood, but insufficient quantities. After a thorough search of state timber depots, enough wood was finally located, but the necessary permits were not granted. He also discovered that the weathering of wood in state timber depots was not done mechanically and often resulted in wood splitting. Because of these problems, the order could not be filled.

The second case deals with a Colombo entrepreneur, who held a series of overseas exhibitions of batik products. Over time, he was able to penetrate a large number of international markets and, by 1983, had established a sizable business. Shortly after this, however, his exports declined, and eventually he was forced to close. Despite a promising start, he faced the following problems:

- Loss of the right to purchase raw materials from government supply outlets;
- An increase in the price of premium quality dye from LKR 9 to 180 per kilogram;
- An increase in the price of poplin from LKR 2.7 to 35.5 per metre;
- An increase in the price of a truckload of firewood from LKR 70 to 1400;
- High interest rates on bank loans; and
- Competition on the international market from low-quality, cheaper products.

Future Perceptions

A majority of craft workers in four out of the six villages do not plan to have their children continue in the trade (Table 24). The exceptions in Kalapura and Molagoda represent villages where incomes are the highest and demand is secure. In the other four villages, however, as with 43% of the respondents in Kalapura and 37% in Molagoda, respondents have other plans. Part of the rationale for this decision has already been explained (see sections on employment and the organization of labour). An additional factor, which also operates in high-income craft villages, is the desire to raise a family's social status by joining the civil service or the private sector or by pursuing an education. Parents believe that educational achievement in the formal school system and work within the government bureaucracy could bring social recognition and status to their caste group and to the region as a whole. In short, artisans want to achieve both economic prosperity and social recognition simul-

Table 24. Artisans' aspirations for their children (%).

	Pahala Beligalla (N = 49)	Embekke (N = 36)	Kalapura (N = 31)	Helambawa-tawana Sengal Oya (N = 30)	Kumbalgama (N = 21)	Molagoda (N = 40)
Should children continue in craft production?						
Yes	23	7	57	33	22	50
No	77	93	43	40	78	37
Not relevant	—	—	—	27	—	13
If "No," why not?						
Work is drudgery	33	14	17	33	9	24
Dislike the work	20	25	—	33	9	
Pursue education and take salaried job	11	28	50	25	—	41
Income is insufficient	27	17	25	—	9	18
Lack of social recognition	—	14	—	—	—	—
Others	9	3	8	8	73	18

taneously. In many of these villages; income from craft production is considerably higher than that earned by a salaried bureaucrat. On the other hand, government work brings social recognition.

Evaluation and Recommendations

National Policy

No explicit policy or rationale for promoting craft production exists. Because there is also no commonly accepted definition, policymakers have been unable to agree on what the craft sector is. In view of research data that cast doubt on the viability of rural production units, this issue must be resolved.

It is difficult to imagine efficient planning taking place in the absence of statistics, particularly employment data. The data base must be improved.

Although the government has promoted small enterprise as a means of improving village welfare, this aim is not shared by local extension agents. Research finds that these workers have paid virtually no attention to artisans, because they believe that rural development should be based on agriculture and that the small-industry sector is of little importance. There is a clear bias toward medium and large-scale enterprises. The goals of the government and of agents implementing government policy should be coordinated.

Government Intervention

Among the six villages studied, there were no examples of support to craft workers from the private sector. This is generally true throughout the country for most craft products. As a result, the government historically has played an important role in assisting artisans. In each village, there were examples of government intervention.

In two villages, government intervention came via organized action by craft workers who eventually secured raw materials and improved marketing facilities, housing, and education. In both cases, artisans aligned themselves with a successful political party and had sufficient votes to make their influence felt. However, smaller artisan communities are generally leaderless and outside the mainstream of political influence. Who will speak for them?

There are many examples of training programs that do not respond to market needs. This has wasted human and financial resources and has led to the production of goods that cannot be sold.

There are also many examples of technology transfer workshops that have not been adequately planned and where equipment is idle. Again, this is a result of inadequate research into the demand for new equipment.

The results of new product development carried out by state institutions flow back to state-supported training and production centres. There is a need to tap the knowledge of the urban private sector and of rural entrepreneurs to bring them into the mainstream of this activity, perhaps by subsidizing their involvement.

The government could provide a useful service by carrying out market studies of the middle class, which has emerged as a significant force in the purchase of locally made products. At present no such surveys exist.

Rural producers have great difficulty in forming links with urban retailers. Many producers are anxious to establish subcontracting arrangements, but do not have the necessary contacts. This would be a useful area of activity for village extension agents.

Demand

There is considerable scope for expansion into overseas markets. Exports grew by over 300% during 1980–83, partly as a result of new market penetration and aggressive marketing by large firms. On the other hand, poor-quality products, resulting from the use of inappropriate materials have led to a loss of markets. However, if steps can be taken to improve quality, some of these markets might be regained. There are examples of new entrepreneurs who have successfully penetrated the export business by keeping overheads low during the initial years of expansion, by carefully studying the market, and by taking full advantage of government export incentives and assistance. There is no reason why others cannot follow this example.

In terms of local demand, the middle class has emerged as a major purchaser of craft products. As stated, however, market surveys are required. The emergence of this class will also help to offset the loss of tourist revenues.

Future Viability

There are serious doubts about the long-term viability of rural artisans producing for the local market. An appraisal of the situation is urgently needed by policymakers. Data indicate that three issues must be addressed.

- Although incomes for rural craft workers are well above the national average and higher than those of agriculturalists, there are more people leaving the trade than entering it. One reason is the lack of confidence in future demand for their skills. In one village with over 50 families producing crafts, only two young people were involved; the remainder were elderly.

- There is a clear desire by parents to see their children take government jobs or work in the private sector. As a result, even in villages where demand is strong, young people are not entering the craft industries. Employment in other occupations providing a monetary wage is seen as a key mechanism for improving a village's social standing.

- Products studied relied on the use of unpaid family labour. However, young people want to earn a monetary wage and decrease their dependence on the family. The traditional system of production is therefore rejected by the younger generation. Data also indicate that some of the young people could be retained in the trade if they were employed in workshops or formally organized industrial units where there was a secure monetary wage.

Some of the most disturbing evidence from Sri Lanka relates to the low self-perception of artisans. This has translated into an inability of the trade to attract new practitioners. Among the countries studied in Asia, this issue of social acceptability was most pronounced in Sri Lanka. Research shows that there is an urgent need for the government to address this problem.

India

Among Asian craft-producing countries, India is unique in a number of key respects. First, both employment and trade generated by this sector are considerable; in most other countries, economic contribution tends to be in only one of these areas. Second, the government has a set of policies in place for the promotion of the small-scale industrial sector, including crafts. These policies have been evident since the early 1950s, whereas most neighbouring countries have only recently adopted such policies. Third, India is one of the few countries in Asia that has policies for both the protection of craft products and their promotion. Although the effectiveness of these policies may well be questioned, at least the need for them has been recognized. Finally, this is the only country where we can see nationwide changes in the craft industry over a period of time, due to the availability of time-series data. The Economic and Establishment Tables incorporated within censuses provide some idea of the magnitude, structure, and changes in the unorganized sector from 1961 to 1981.

This chapter draws together already available macro data on craft employment, production, and trade, along with the results of field surveys carried out among

Table 25. Products and locations covered in the field survey.

Craft	Number of artisans	Locations
Wood and stone carving	237	Saharanpur, Hoshiarpur, Mysore, Bangalore, Sorab, Sirsi, Sagar, Delhi, Channapattna, Sankheda, Jaipur, Agra
Carpet making	233	Jaipur, Mirzapur, Kashmir, Bhadoi, Agra
Metal work	98	Moradabad, Jaipur, Bidar, Varanasi
Embroidery	51	Saurashtra, Srinagar, Lucknow
Gems and jewelry	38	Jaipur, Cambay, Udupi, Varanasi, Delhi, Patan, Mau Nath, Bhanjan

700 artisans throughout the country (Jain 1986). Five major groups of crafts were studied at the household level during 1983–85 (Table 25). Analysis concentrates on three issues: national employment and foreign exchange earnings; changes in the structure of this industry over time; and a review of policy and government support programs.

National Trends in Employment, Job Creation, and Production

Not only are there large numbers of artisans working in India, but there have also been drastic increases in new jobs created. In 1955, a landmark study done for the government on craft marketing estimated that there were 1 million artisans in the country (Indian Cooperative Union 1955). Between 1961 and 1981, 2.43 million new jobs were created in this sector (Table 26). Equally interesting are the data for the

Table 26. Increases in craft employment, 1961–81.

Sector	Number of new jobs ('000)
Craft sector	
Jewelry	484
Carpets	223
Embroidery	101
Basketry (cane, bamboo)	609
Earthenware and pottery[a]	115
Other crafts such as wood carving, metal, etc.	500
Marginal workers (estimated at 20% of main workers)	406
Total	2428
Organized sector	
Public sector	1163
Private sector	1525
Total	2688

[a] This relates only to the period 1971–81. It is likely that there were also additions to employment in this craft between 1961 and 1971.

Source: Census and economic surveys.

entire industrial sector, which show that the number of new jobs created in crafts is comparable to the total created by both private and public firms in the organized sector (2.43 million compared to 2.69 million).

Although data on the value of production are not entirely reliable or adequate, estimates show a steady increase in absolute terms, from INR 1000 million (in 1988, 14 Indian rupees (INR) = 1 United States dollar (USD)) in 1955 to INR 37 500 million in 1983–84 (Report on the marketing of handicrafts, Raj Krishna Committee). However a slight decrease in output per person has occurred in recent years.

Employment Trends by Product

Carpets and Jewelry

Together, these two products accounted for 708 766 new jobs between 1961 and 1981 (Tables 27 and 28). Jewelry showed an increase of 156% and carpets 274%.

Virtually all workers are male: in jewelry the percentage is 98% and in carpets 92%. Over this 20-year period, the ratio of men to women in jewelry remained the same, whereas in carpets, employment for women has decreased. In 1961 their share was 15%, but this declined to 8% in 1981 even though 223 087 new jobs were created.

There has been an obvious shift in the production of jewelry from rural to urban areas: 44% was urban in 1961, but 64% in 1981. Carpet production, however, has been growing in the opposite direction. In 1961, 78% of production took place in the

Table 27. Changes in employment in jewelry (main workers) from 1961 to 1981.

	1981		1971		1961	Change, 1961 to 1981	
	Number	%	Number	%	Number	Number	%
Total	796 392[a]	100	540 901	100	310 713	485 679	156
Male	783 831	98		98			
Female	12 561	2		2			
Urban	507 021	64		44			
Male	499 480						
Female	7 541						
Household industry	230 087	29		63			
Male	224 594						
Female	5 493						
Urban	117 168						
Male	113 969						
Female	3 199						
Nonhousehold industry	566 305	71		37			
Male	559 237						
Female	7 068						
Urban	398 933						
Male	385 511						
Female	4 422						

[a] According to the 1981 Industrial Classification, employment in jewelry was 796 392. However, the 1981 Occupational Classification (Group 88) shows employment in jewelry and precious metals or metal engraving (except printing) somewhat higher at 841 154.
Source: Census surveys. There are minor discrepancies between the sum of the subtotals and the grand total.

Table 28. Changes in employment in the carpet industry (main workers), 1961–81.

	1981		1961		Change, 1961 to 1981	
	Number	%	Number	%	Number	%
Total	304 499	100	81 412	100	223 087	274
Male	279 466	92	69 246	85	210 220	303
Female	25 032	8	12 166	15	12 866	106
Rural	254 302	84	60 001	78	194 301	324
Male	233 203		50 386		182 817	363
Female	21 099		9 615		11 484	119
Household						
industry	194 852	64	56 213	69	138 639	247
Male	176 180		44 976		131 204	292
Female	18 672		11 237		7 435	66
Rural	166 873		45 383		121 490	268
Male	150 751		36 321		114 430	315
Female	16 122		9 062		7 060	78
Urban	27 979		10 830		17 149	158
Male	25 429		8 655		16 774	194
Female	2 550		2 175		375	17
Nonhousehold						
industry	109 647	36	25 190	31	84 457	335
Male	103 287		24 202		79 085	327
Female	6 360		928		5 432	585
Rural	87 429		14 617		72 812	498
Male	82 452		14 004		68 448	489
Female	4 977		553		4 424	800
Urban	22 228		10 573		11 655	110
Male	20 835		10 198		10 637	104
Female	1 393		375		1 018	271

Source: Census surveys.

country; in 1981 this climbed to 84%. This is essentially where the increase in new jobs occurred.

In jewelry, manufacturing has moved away from household units, where in 1961 it represented 63% of production, to only 29% in 1981. The figures for carpets have remained fairly stable.

Embroidery

Embroidery and similar textile goods accounted for an additional 101 833 jobs (Table 29), but, surprisingly, men filled most of these new positions. Furthermore, 16 140 women who had previously been employed in these occupations found their work taken away by men.

There was a significant change in the proportion of jobs undertaken in the home. The household industry segment dropped from 60% to 33% during the 20 years from 1961 to 1981.

Bamboo and Cane

Within the craft sector, these products accounted for the largest number of new jobs. During 1961–81, employment rose by 608 964, all in the category of full-time

Table 29. Changes in employment in embroidery, knitting, and lace making (main workers), 1961–81.

	1981		1961		Change, 1961 to 1981	
	Number	%	Number	%	Number	%
Total	242 707	100	140 874	100	101 833	72
Male	198 311	82	80 328	57	117 983	147
Female	44 406	18	60 546	43	− 16 140	− 26
Urban	154 518	64	78 65	56	75 862	96
Male	131 311		57 351		73 960	129
Female	23 207		21 305		1 902	9
Household						
industry	79 345	33	84 858	60	− 5 513	− 6
Male	55 732		33 734		21 998	65
Female	23 612		51 124		− 27 512	− 54
Urban	35 102		37 962		− 2 860	− 54
Male	25 542		12 392		13 150	106
Female	9 560		19 570		− 10 010	− 51
Nonhousehold						
industry	159 791	66	54 644	39	105 147	192
Male	139 912		45 491		94 421	208
Female	19 879		9 153		10 726	117
Urban	116 640		44 974		71 666	159
Male	103 652		38 977		64 675	166
Female	12 987		5 997		6 990	117

Source: Census surveys.

Table 30. Changes in employment in bamboo, cane, and rattan (main workers), 1961–81.

	1981		1971		1961	Change, 1961 to 1981	
	Number	%	Number	%	Number	Number	%
Total	905 807	100	516 655	100	296 843	608 964	205
Male	544 114	69	347 735	67			
Female	361 693	40	168 831	33			
Rural	729 791	81	405 705	79			
Male	425 333		268 475				
Female	304 453		137 590				
Household							
industry	706 950	78					
Male	404 410						
Female	302 540						
Rural	602 314						
Male	343 595						
Female	258 718						
Nonhousehold							
industry	198 857	22					
Male	139 704						
Female	59 153						
Rural	127 477						
Male	81 737						
Female	45 741						

Source: Census surveys.

workers (Table 30). Furthermore, this growth was steady throughout the 20-year period. Production in the rural areas was sustained and even improved slightly, from 79% in 1971 to 81% in 1981.

Table 31. Changes in employment in earthenware and pottery (main workers), 1971–81.

	1981		1971		Change, 1971 to 1981	
	Number	%	Number	%	Number	%
Total	682 697	100	568 076	100	114 621	20
Male	537 172	79	470 695	83	66 477	14
Female	144 925	21	97 381	17	47 544	49
Rural	565 988	83	491 884	87	74 104	15
Male	443 814		406 721		37 093	9
Female	121 574		85 163		36 411	43

Source: Census surveys.

This is one of the few industries where employment for women increased and, it should be noted, not at the expense of male employment. Jobs for women rose from 168 831 to 361 693 or 114% from 1971 to 1981 (Table 30). Furthermore, most of this increase took place in the rural areas and within the home. This industry has emerged as an important source of income for rural women.

Pottery and Earthenware

Between 1971 and 1981, this industry absorbed 114 621 new workers and is overwhelmingly male dominated: 83% in 1971 and 79% in 1981 (Table 31). Employment for women improved slightly from 17% to 21%, which represents 47 544 new jobs. The industry remains primarily rural, with 87% of total employment in the country. Of the additional 114 621 jobs created, 74 104 were in rural areas.

Trends in Foreign Exchange Earnings

Growth in exports has been as impressive as the creation of employment. Earnings from craft exports grew from a negligible level in 1961 to INR 16 700 million in 1983–84 and now accounts for 16% of India's trade (Table 32). In fact, in 1978–79 exchange earnings from craft exports were greater than the total of all foreign-aid disbursements for that year (ILO 1983). The most export-intensive products have been gems and jewelry, followed by carpets, textiles, and wood. The main markets are the United States, West Germany, the Soviet Union, and the Middle East. (For additional information on India's exports, please see the case study, Indian Craft Exports for the Global Market (Kathuria 1988).)

Changes in the Craft Industry Since 1955

Important changes have been taking place in this industry since 1955 as a result of strong export and domestic demand. However, although employment has risen dramatically, in some cases this change has not been beneficial to the artisan. Unless corrective action is taken, there may be serious problems in the long term, with an inevitable decline in exports and subsequent unemployment. The analysis presented here is based on census data as well as field studies among 700 craftsmen throughout the country.

Table 32. Value of craft exports, 1961 to 1984.

	Value of exports (INR 10 million)[a]			
	1961–62	1971–72	1981–82	1983–84[b]
Gems and jewelry	9.04 (46.7)[c]	52.28 (57.8)	807.11 (66.2)	1323.96 (79.3)
Other crafts	10.30 (53.3)	38.24 (42.2)	412.13 (33.8)	345.81 (20.7)
Wool carpets	4.42	13.69	173.48	147.69
Metal	1.48	7.12	95.86	67.23
Wood	0.32	3.05	20.25	10.96
Hand-printed textiles	1.16	4.50	39.67	33.38
Cotton carpets	0.01	0.82	11.44	18.30
Miscellaneous crafts	2.91	9.06	71.43	68.25
Total craft exports	19.34 (100)	90.52 (100)	1219.25 (100)	1669.78 (100)
Craft exports as % of total exports Including gems and jewelry	—[d]	5	15	16
Excluding gems and jewelry	—	2	5	4

[a] In 1988, 14 Indian rupees (INR) = 1 USD.
[b] 1983–84 figures are estimates.
[c] Figures in parentheses are percentages of the total.
[d] —, negligible.
Source: Directorate-General of Commercial Intelligence and Statistics, monthly statistics of foreign trade.

Employment, Exports, and Production Levels

Employment in the craft sector increased from 1 million in 1955 to 3.5 million in 1981. The number of new jobs created in this industry is comparable to the total amount of additional employment in the organized industrial sector, both public and private. Growth in export production has been concentrated in gems and jewelry, carpets, metal and wood products, and embroidery. On the domestic side, employment has increased most in bamboo, cane, and pottery. Exports were "negligible" in 1961, but increased to 16% of India's trade in 1982–83 with a value of INR 16 700 million (Table 32). Production increased from INR 20 500 million in 1979–80 to INR 32 000 million in 1984–85.

Composition of Trade

Large export levels obscure the fact that trade is concentrated in relatively few products, which in turn are sold in a limited market. This indicates a significant opportunity for trade expansion in the future, as well as a current failure of marketing channels.

Structural Change

Products for domestic use are still largely made by household units located in the rural areas. These industries are also more favourable to women's employment. However, export-led industries show significant change. They have shifted toward urban centres and the nonhousehold sector. In addition, data indicate that they provide limited opportunities for women.

61

The Traditional Production System

It is clear that the traditional pattern of production is undergoing considerable stress. Historically, goods were made for certain key periods of demand, such as religious occasions, festivals, and marriages. This allowed production to take place in an orderly fashion, and artisans could stock products in advance with little risk. Although exports have brought new opportunities, they have also upset the established order. Now, artisans are faced with cyclical or uncertain demand from overseas, but have few resources at their disposal to overcome this problem.

International trade has also led to a more organized industry because export producers gravitate to the city. As a result, much of the decision-making process has passed from the artisan to the manufacturer, whose primary interest is sales, not the welfare of the craft worker. This pursuit of short-term gains can have a detrimental effect on both the artisans and their products. Given the size of India's exports, policy intervention is necessary to ensure an orderly transition of the industry, to minimize hardships placed on producers, and to provide for the long-term survival of these products.

Training

Large gains in exports within a short period of time have strained the hereditary system of skills transfer which functioned well when demand was evenly spread. As a result, skill levels and quality have decreased. Although a supply of good workers remains, field evidence shows that unless remedial steps are taken, this talent will disappear over time, with disastrous results.

Under the traditional system, artisans assume the financial responsibility for training a younger generation. These costs are considerable. For many crafts, a number of years are required to master a particular skill (Table 33). However, with the escalating cost of living, many artisans are finding that they cannot meet this obligation. Although the data can be interpreted in various ways, this is one reason why 50% of the 72 artisan families interviewed do not plan to teach their children a craft trade.

Division of Labour

Among the products studied, especially textiles, metal work, and carpets, there is considerable division of labour in the production process. Workers are typically taught a very limited range of skills, and there are no attempts being made to expand

Table 33. Time required to learn a skill for selected crafts.

	Up to 1 year	1–2 years	2–4 years	4–6 years	Over 6 years
Rosewood carving	—	—	—	7	1
Sandalwood carving	—	14	40	12	5
Metal work	1	16	21	3	—
Lacquerware	26	—	4	—	—
Silver jewelry	—	—	5	5	8
Total (and percent)	27 (16.1)	30 (17.9)	70 (41.7)	27 (16.1)	14 (8.3)

this range. Even in government training programs, such as that for carpet making, workers are taught only one skill. Research indicates that this is dangerous as it greatly limits job mobility and may leave the worker open to long periods of unemployment. This system can also create imbalances in the supply of specialized skills. Research shows that this is already happening.

Guidance on Designs

Although the traditional system is being uprooted, in most cases there is no alternative mechanism in place to provide advice on designs. Historically, this was done by the individual artisan who was inspired by his cultural background. Today, products are being mass-produced for the export market, with a decline in quality and a loss of traditional motifs. It is a reasonable assumption that China's recognition of this is one reason for her large growth in exports. A recent study concludes:

> China also has quality and delivery problems, but we found its reputation to be much higher than India's. A big advantage that it has over India is that production is undertaken in factories in a controlled environment, which makes quality and delivery more reliable. (Kathuria and Taneja 1986, p. 45)

It is clear that the role of design has not been adequately appreciated in the marketing chain. Designs are one means of protecting a cultural heritage and simultaneously enter new markets. The private sector is often either unwilling or unable to invest in this aspect of production. Yet, virtually all studies indicate that this is a critical part of production and imperative for increased sales, especially in the export market. Sanjay Kathuria's study on exports markets (Kathuria 1988) indicates that among 94 exporters and importers interviewed, only five were actually involved in design and development work. All five were importing firms.

Market Intelligence

Collection of information on markets, both export and domestic, could be significantly improved. For example, neither government export development corporations nor domestic sales emporia have a systematic mechanism for gathering marketing information.

Technology

Investigations in the field found no evidence that support is being provided for the use of improved technologies, or that provisions are being made to protect workers from occupational hazards. Among 72 artisan families studied, all changes in technology came as a result of their own efforts. Although technological adaptation by individuals without outside intervention can be highly useful, this can only be carried so far. Health hazards, for example, which are considerable in metal and wood work, cannot be adequately dealt with by rural workers.

Wages

The wage intensity of different products varies enormously (Table 34). In some cases, wages represent a very high percentage of the total value of a product (e.g., densely knotted wool carpets), while for others raw material costs are the significant

Table 34. Wage intensity of various craft products.

Product	Share of cost (%)[a]	
	Raw materials	Wages
Handknotted wool carpets		
46 080 knots/m²	58.3	38.3
76 800 "	45.6	47.9
134 400 "	42.1	52.1
207 360 "	37.7	62.2
244 944 "	23.3	74.6
333 396 "	14.4	84.1
Wool fabrics		
1.5 × 6 m 60s	64.0	36.0
90 × 120 cm 30s	69.5	30.5
Embroidery (sarees, 5.5 m)		
Cotton	50.4	43.6
Silk	65.4	25.7
Georgette	68.2	23.8
Metal ware		
Brass planters	63	37
Brass flower vases	59	41

[a] Percentages may not total 100% because other costs, e.g. interest, are involved.

factor (e.g., embroidered silk sarees). There is no attempt being made to maximize gains for the artisan.

Large gains in export trade have not been adequately shared with artisans. Although exporters' margins are sufficient to absorb escalating costs of raw materials or a fall in demand, wages are the first cost item to be reduced. This practice must be considered with respect to the consumer price index. Although we found increases in wages over time, these increases have not always kept pace with the price index. For example, the Agra carpet industry suffered a sudden drop in demand during the early 1980s, leading to a reduction of 32% in the selling price. Wages were subsequently reduced INR 900 to 600 for a 1.8 × 1.2 m wool carpet of 11 × 19 knots per inch² (1 inch² = 6.3 cm²). During the same period, the cost of wool increased by 20%. In response, exporters took a cut in their margin from INR 470 in 1978 to INR 140 in 1983 which, nevertheless, is still a comfortable return. For workers, however, the drop of INR 300 was a disaster, because during this same period the consumer price index rose by 173 points (from 324 in 1977 to 497 in 1983 with 1960 as the base). Because 92% of all Agra's carpets are made for export, workers had no alternative but to accept wage reductions. Similar situations have been found elsewhere in India. In short, a disproportionate amount of risk seems to be borne by the artisan himself.

The concern expressed here about wages is supported by other research in India. One study among rural artisans in Karnataka found that 70% of all craft workers were below the poverty line (Abdul Aziz 1980). In addition, the All-India Debt and Investment Survey (1971–72) showed that rural households with an artisan head-of-household had a much lower net wealth than other families, and that 99% were landless as against 36% for other sectors of the population.

Cooperatives

The history of cooperatives in India has generally been a troubled one, and perhaps for this reason there is now little evidence of an institutional base at the worker's level that can protect artisans and promote their interests. (For an evaluation of India's experience with cooperatives in craft production, see Taimni (1981).) In 1980, cooperatives accounted for less than 1% of total craft production, and only 2% of the country's artisans work within a cooperative arrangement. Nevertheless, some structure is necessary to provide a decent standard of living and to cope with the pressures of cyclical demand, escalating material prices, etc. As has been well documented in a recent study on rural development under government planning in India, "*Ideas* need appropriate *institutions* to fulfill their social promise" (Jain et al. 1985, p. 203).

Policy and the Craft Sector

State Support

Each development plan has stressed the importance to national economic welfare of village and small-scale industry, of which crafts are a part. The emphasis has been on the ability of these small units to absorb labour, increase export earnings, and preserve skills. Except for the Second and Third Plans when the village and small-scale industries sectors received 4% and 2.8%, respectively, their share has always been less than 2% (Table 35). Within these two sectors, the share given to crafts has been nominal: 3.2%, 2.4%, and 2% in the first three Plans, and 3.85% and 6.23% in the Fifth and Sixth Plans. The total expenditure on crafts from the First through the Sixth Plan has been less than INR 1400 million.

In contrast, between 1960 and 1984, the craft industry earned INR 95 160 million in foreign exchange and provided 250 000 new jobs. As noted earlier, foreign exchange earnings from crafts now account for 16% of total trade. Furthermore, additional employment in crafts has almost equaled that of the entire organized industrial sector.

There are certainly grounds for questioning the wisdom of plan allocations. As a report from this study states:

> The resources and attention received by the handicraft sector, relative to its contribution to employment and foreign exchange at the hands of the Plan, bear no comment.

Table 35. Share of Plan expenditures for village and small-industry sector compared with expenditures for industry and minerals.

Plan	Expenditures on village and small industrial sectors		Expenditures on industry and minerals (%)
	INR[a] million	%	
First, 1951–56	430	2.0	2.8
Second, 1956–61	1 800	4.0	19.6
Third, 1961–66	2 410	2.8	20.1
1966–69	1 260	1.9	22.8
Fourth, 1969–74	2 420	1.5	18.2
Fifth, 1974–78	3 880	1.3	24.0
Sixth			
Draft, 1978–83	14 100	1.8	19.7
1980–85	17 800	1.8	13.6

Source: Plan documents and economic survey.
[a]In 1988, 14 Indian rupees (INR) = 1 USD.

What bears comment, however, is that some of the acute problems of craftsmen — of (1) working and living space, (2) health facilities, (3) orderly supply of raw materials, (4) relief from the burden of training skilled workers which is now entirely on their lean shoulders, and (5) some cushion against trade risks . . . cry for attention. (Jain 1986, p. 881)

To complete our understanding of the craft sector in India and implications for policy, it is useful to look at the most recent census data for the entire unorganized industrial sector. Although there are limitations to this data, the following conclusions may be drawn.

Employment in household industries declined by 36% during 1961–81. In the rural areas, this decline was 45%. The most dramatic decline took place in rural households employing women (Table 36).

Of the additional 3 700 000 new jobs created in rural areas under the classification nonhousehold industries, men took two-thirds and women one-third.

There are a great many units, both organized and unorganized, that are operating without electrical power. The number of such industries has been increasing and now employs 6 500 000 people. The vast majority of rural-based household units operate without power. Of the 3 804 000 workers employed in 1971 in household industries, 2 980 000 were operating without power and 2 932 000 were located in rural areas. These figures clearly reveal an inability on the part of the developmental system to provide power; they raise serious doubts about the capacity of small industrial units to improve productivity and efficiency on their own.

Recommendations

• The overall data base should be improved to include, for example, more reliable estimates on annual production. Furthermore, state efforts in collecting data must be improved, as it is primarily the state's responsibility to collect data on such issues as employment.

• The infrastructure should be extended into rural areas so that electrical power becomes more widely available.

Table 36. Changes in employment in household and nonhousehold industries from 1961 to 1981.

	Employment ('000)		
	1961	1981	% change
Household industries			
Rural areas	9 900	5 400	−46
Women workers	4 700	2 100	−55
Women in rural areas	3 900	1 500	−62
Total	12 000	7 700	−36
Nonhousehold industries			
Rural areas	2 400	6 100	154
Women workers	800	1 600	100
Women in rural areas	400	800	100
Total	8 000	17 400	118

Source: Census data.

- An institutional base should be established for providing raw materials, training, and marketing assistance.

- Training subsidies should be provided without supplanting the traditional system of skills transfer, so that current costs can be reduced.

- An improvement should be made in housing and work space for artisans, especially those whose production process is space intensive, such as carpet weavers.

- Improvements in tools and the overall production process should include designs on a large enough scale to cover a substantial portion of the work force.

- Plan allocations to crafts should be increased so that national spending is commensurate with this sector's contributions to trade and employment.

- Protection from factory competition should be provided for a wide range of products that are experiencing severe problems from loss of competitive edge. This study found that hand-woven carpets, hand-printed textiles, brass and bell-metal utensils, silk, hand-embroidered products, and hand-made pottery are all facing severe competition from factory-made substitutes. This point has been made repeatedly since 1955, but there is not much evidence that it has been acted upon.

Thailand

The craft economy of Thailand can be divided into two segments, both large and important in their own right. The strong demand for exports has led to a heavy concentration of large factories and workshops in major metropolitan centres such as Bangkok and Chiangmai. The vast majority of the country's craft exports come from a few large urban cities such as these. Although export orders are still made in semi-rural areas through subcontracting arrangements, the cities remain focal points for overseas trade. These centres are increasing in importance, as exports continue to grow at a rapid pace. Overseas sales increased by an average of 38% per year between 1970 and 1982. In addition to urban producers working for the export market, the country also has a large number of small, part-time rural artisans who are primarily farmers, but who draw on craft income to supplement agricultural earnings. Nationally, Thailand has very high levels of nonfarm income, averaging 40% for all farm families. Earnings from crafts are a major source of such income. Although national employment data on the artisan sector are unavailable, one World Bank study estimated that there were 460 000 households with looms in Thailand alone in 1979 (World Bank 1983, p. 140).

Although craft income is critical for low income farmers, with craft earnings representing up to 50% of total household income, many rural artisan industries are being phased out. For example, between 1968–69 and 1975–76 the number of households owning hand looms and mat machines declined in all parts of the country except Bangkok, where the number of looms increased, no doubt as a result of the export trade (World Bank 1983, p. 80). This decline is in direct contrast to trends in urban areas. With respect to rural artisans, a World Bank report states: "We can expect an almost total disappearance of these activities in the near future" (World Bank 1983, p. 82). The future viability of artisan products in both rural and urban areas, as well as those catering to different markets, requires a critical study drawing on field evidence.

Hopefully this report on the weaving, wood, and wicker industries in Lamphun and Chiangmai provinces will cast some light on these issues. Although research was not carried out in Bangkok, studies were made of wood exporters in Chiangmai, one of the major urban centres in the north. Among rural producers, wicker manufacturers and cotton weavers were studied (Table 37). Although this research took place in only two northern provinces, its findings will nevertheless shed light on the problems and prospects facing both rural and urban producers on a nationwide basis.

The upper northern portion of Thailand where this research was conducted is the country's poorest area. It can be characterized as small-holder agricultural, with a large landless population. The average farm size is the smallest in the country. Not surprisingly, average incomes are also the lowest, at THB 14 021 (in 1988, 25 Thai baht (THB) = 1 United States dollar (USD)). Nonagricultural income,

Table 37. Sample size for Chiangmai and Lamphun research project.

	Chiangmai			Lamphun			
	Wicker	Weaving	Wood	Wicker	Weaving	Wood	Total
Total craft households[a]	18 036	10 401	2 525	9 701	4 871	1 132	46 666
Project sample							
Subcontracted workers	100	140	130	45	85	30	530
Self-employed	40	—	—	20	—	—	60
Entrepreneurs	10	10	15	10	10	15	70
Middlemen	10	10	10	5	3	2	40
Raw material suppliers	5	5	5	5	3	2	25
Policymakers							20[b]
Total sample	165	165	160	85	101	49	745

[a] Numerated from the *Handicraft village directories of Chiangmai and Lamphun provinces*, which was produced by this research project.
[b] Ten from each province.

therefore, is extremely important and represents 50% of total household income (World Bank 1983, p. 41).

As far as existing knowledge of Thai artisans is concerned, the situation is similar in some respects to that of other Asian countries. There has never been a national study of this industry, and this is the first regional research report. National data on employment and production are lacking. In the field of rural industrialization, there have been more studies in Thailand than in other countries as a result of the government's strong push in recent national Plans to develop nonfarm employment. As a result, the data base has improved, although it is still far from adequate. The more significant studies have been done by the International Labour Organization's Asian Regional Team for Employment Promotion (ARTEP), in response to requests from the country's planning commission, and by a consortium of universities, primarily Kasetsart University, funded by the United States Agency for International Development (USAID). These have been of particular value to this current study. However, there is no substitute for industry-specific research, and in the case of crafts, aside from a few isolated case studies, nothing has been available until now.

Contributions to National Economic Development

Employment

Unfortunately, the periodic Socio-Economic Surveys do not test for craft employment, except for textile workers. For example, they do not estimate part-time employment, especially when work is undertaken in the home by women. National figures as such are unavailable, and even conjectures cannot be made. In the two provinces studied, craft employment, both full- and part-time, amounted to 7% of the labour force: in wicker, there were 27 740 households involved; in wood, 3360 households; and in weaving, 15 272 households. Because this upper northern region, in addition to the northeast, is the main location for artisan activities in the country, these figures will be higher than for other areas of the nation. For example, in the south, major employers are the rubber industry and fisheries, areas of work not open to those living in the north. As a result, there are fewer artisans in the south. Estimates of the number of artisan workers in metropolitan Bangkok are also not available. This lack national data and data for major urban centres is a major drawback to those engaged in long-range planning.

Exports

Export statistics (Table 38) show that, unlike most commodities for which fluctuations are common, craft exports have increased every year since records were kept in 1970. Increases have not been gradual, but have climbed an average of 38% per year from THB 214 million in 1970 to THB 8.5 billion in 1982. There is a predictable concentration in the gems and jewelry category, with these sales amounting to approximately 50% of the total. The remaining sales are evenly spread among leather, wood, textiles, and metal products. Despite these encouraging signs, total craft exports reached only 0.054% of total exports in 1982. Although this shows room for improvement, the THB 8.5 billion in craft exports in 1982 in some measure offset a trade deficit of THB 36 billion in that same year. A major push is now being made by the government to increase exports in all areas, as the trade deficit increased dangerously to THB 69 billion in 1984.

Table 38. Value of craft exports 1970–82 (THB^a million).

Categories	1970	1971	1972	1973	1974	1975	1976	1977	1978	1979	1980	1981	1982
Precious stones	115.0	221.8	361.1	628.7	760.0	781.3	783.7	1051.7	1699.1	2230.4	3220.7	4465.7	4645.0
Leather products	0.4	0.6	7.3	23.3	56.7	40.6	78.0	189.4	379.5	733.9	717.0	830.6	1059.8
Wood and carved wood products	25.8	50.3	104.5	211.9	256.1	292.9	358.4	438.0	548.0	719.5	694.0	696.4	743.0
Jewelry and ornaments	7.2	8.4	14.7	41.7	41.9	47.5	63.8	132.8	258.6	324.0	443.1	434.2	466.4
Wooden and carved furniture	0.2	0.5	1.5	15.2	36.6	31.1	33.7	52.2	96.9	185.1	226.1	292.4	336.8
Rattan furniture	0.1	0.3	1.1	10.4	23.9	22.5	26.6	40.0	75.7	141.9	231.5	314.2	346.8
Silk	35.8	33.1	32.8	44.2	40.1	33.5	36.7	38.6	47.4	53.9	90.2	155.5	175.5
Bronzeware	15.0	12.5	18.8	30.1	37.3	42.5	49.6	59.2	77.9	93.0	166.8	54.1	115.3
Silver and nickleware	10.4	13.9	27.8	33.4	40.1	40.1	57.0	74.1	139.5	226.8	162.8	219.4	212.2
Wicker	0.8	0.8	4.2	16.9	32.6	11.8	28.0	33.8	44.5	75.7	144.0	117.3	115.1
Handwoven cotton textiles	0.9	2.5	6.3	20.8	23.7	27.2	42.6	38.5	47.9	60.8	79.5	84.8	92.4
Artificial flowers and fruit	0.3	0.3	0.5	2.2	5.5	6.1	12.2	25.9	30.2	41.9	72.8	98.0	94.1
Paintings and sculptures	0.5	2.2	9.3	23.2	52.4	22.6	2.3	5.3	11.9	34.7	38.4	12.4	17.5
Metal castings and statuettes	—	—	—	—	—	0.3	6.1	15.6	24.9	22.6	26.3	54.1	65.2
Pearl, ivory, horn, and bone products	0.1	0.6	4.4	6.5	10.8	25.2	33.6	41.1	39.1	34.2	25.5	14.6	11.7
Ceramic products	1.0	1.1	1.5	3.4	0.7	3.4	4.9	9.3	9.8	16.2	24.3	39.7	36.7
Thai dolls	0.3	0.3	0.3	1.4	2.3	1.9	3.3	6.9	5.2	11.8	23.1	27.5	29.9
Lacquerware	n.a.	n.a.	n.a.	n.a.	n.a.	n.a.	n.a.	5.7	6.5	11.3	9.1	7.5	9.4
Umbrellas	—	—	—	—	0.1	0.1	0.6	1.3	3.2	5.9	6.9	6.5	4.8
Other craft products	—	—	—	0.1	0.3	2.3	4.1	8.2	3.8	5.3	8.7	19.7	9.5
Total	213.8	349.1	596.1	1113.4	1421.1	1432.6	1625.2	2267.6	3549.6	5028.9	6410.8	7944.6	8587.1

^{a}In 1988, 25 Thai baht (THB) = 1 USD.
Source: Handicraft Promotion Division, Department of Industrial Promotion.

Government Policy Toward Small-Scale Industries

Industrialization in Thailand has clearly favoured large firms as well as those located in cities, particularly Bangkok. This city's dominance in industrial output is overwhelming; it now accounts for 47% of all manufacturing units in the country (ILO–ARTEP 1985, p. 81). The dominance of large industries is illustrated by the fact that of all firms receiving promotional privileges from the government in 1982, 742 firms, or 94% of the total, had 50 workers or more. The average number of workers per firm was 356 (ILO–ARTEP 1985, p. 76). However, small-scale firms employ more workers: 1 324 438 workers, or 6.2% of the labour force, are employed in small-scale manufacturing; 400 562 or 1.9% work in larger firms. Furthermore, employment has been increasing more rapidly in small enterprises than in large industries. The picture that emerges is one in which large firms receive most of the benefits, but employment and growth are at the small-scale level.

To rectify these imbalances, the last Five Year Plan, covering the period up to October 1986, put considerable emphasis on restructuring the economy to make it more export oriented and diversified in the rural areas. It also identified certain key low-income areas of the country, or "poverty districts," for special employment and income support. Part of the overall objective of this Plan was to address the increasing problem of seasonal unemployment, as the number of people who were out of work during periods of low agricultural activity grew from 4 million in 1978 to 5.5 million in 1982. During this time, the number of underemployed across the country increased from 4.7 million to 8.7 million (Chaiwat Roongruangsee et al. 1985).

The transformation of cottage industries was a key objective in this Plan. Policy was aimed at promoting the expansion of home-based units to enable a larger scale of production and to provide assistance to units that used local raw materials for export. In line with this emphasis, the new Plan for 1987–91 has specified rural industrialization and employment as its key objectives. The attainment of these goals will in large part depend on the government's ability to overcome some very considerable obstacles, such as the reluctance of Bangkok-based entrepreneurs to invest in rural areas, away from their families, supplies, and warehouses. Furthermore, the poverty districts identified for special support are the farthest removed from metropolitan centres and have poor infrastructure. It is not clear precisely what types of new employment can take hold in these locations, although an increased emphasis on the export of crafts is one choice.

Government Support for Artisans

Support for artisans in Thailand has a better record than in most other Asian countries. They receive the active patronage of the Royal Family, and their activities are well publicized by the national media. As a result, the somewhat negative image of this sector, which is a constraint in some other countries, is not a factor in Thailand. In addition, both the government and private sectors are more active than in neighbouring states. Not only is there a specific government agency assigned to the craft sector, but there are also import duties to protect some of the indigenous industries such as silk, ceramics, and carpets. Finally, there also appears to be greater receptivity on the part of both private and public agencies to the idea of working together, especially on export promotion schemes.

The agency within the government for assisting artisans is the Department of Industrial Promotion (DIP) within the Ministry of Industry. Some measure of DIP's important role in overall development efforts can be seen in its budget, which increased by 219%, from 1977 to 1983 (THB 26 million to THB 83 million). Although DIP covers a wide range of industries, 40% of its total allocation goes to cottage and craft industries.

Other government agencies with responsibilities for craft support are:

- Handicraft Promotion Division, DIP (research on raw materials, technology, production; and marketing and promotional activities)

- Board of Investment (tax privileges)

- Department of Customs (reduced duties on raw material imports used for export products; and tariffs placed on ceramics, carpets, jewelry and silk to protect the indigenous industries)

- Small Industries Finance Office, DIP (credit)

- Office of Foreign Trade and the Office of Commercial Relations (export promotion and information on Thai products for overseas buyers)

- Thai Trade Centre (marketing promotion).

Evidence from the Field

Wood, wicker, and cotton products were selected for field study because they are produced by rural-based units making goods for local consumption, as well as by large, city workshops catering to export and tourist markets. Wicker goods are made on a part-time basis by both men and women and almost all villages are involved. Goods are for use in the home, but some are also sold commercially. Orders are often received through subcontracting arrangements. The city of Chiangmai is one of the country's dominant centres for the manufacture of teak furniture, as well as other products made from locally available wood. Work is undertaken in factories sometimes employing up to 350 people. Occasionally, manufacturing is also carried out in village workshops, via subcontracting agreements. However, despite the fact that wood firms are normally larger scale commercial enterprises, their workers come from agricultural families and frequently leave to work on the farm. Cotton weaving is done exclusively by women, on a part- or full-time basis, depending on whether goods are being made for local use or for sale in larger quantities through entrepreneurs serving distant markets. This is one example of a product that has moved toward a larger commercial base as a result of demand from hotels, restaurants, and tourists.

The Link to Agriculture

The relationship between agriculture and craft production is important in these two provinces, because of the heavily agricultural, and subsistence, nature of the economy. Agriculture affects the future potential of the craft industry, and crafts in turn play an important role in household well being.

Because farm incomes are the lowest in the country, many households raise their standard of living by working as artisans (Table 39). In the areas studied, artisan incomes do not represent merely a residual portion of household income, but a very

Table 39. Average annual income of artisan families from various sources.

	Income (THB)[a]				Craft income as % of total
	Agricultural	Non-agricultural[b]	Craft	Total	
Wicker producers					
Chiangmai	13 978	15 930	8 468	29 326	29
Lumphun	8 697	11 226	11 039	22 388	49
Total	12 455	14 723	9 316	27 173	34
Wood carvers					
Chiangmai	10 467	12 401	15 472	30 010	52
Lumphun	8 942	7 665	8 230	20 919	39
Total	10 153	11 431	14 114	28 306	50
Weavers					
Chiangmai	13 117	20 455	6 566	26 819	24
Lumphun	9 593	22 411	10 427	32 063	33
Total	11 869	21 364	8 025	28 800	28

[a] In 1988, 25 Thai baht (THB) = 1 USD.
[b] Other than craft income.

substantial proportion of it: 50, 34, and 28% of total income for wood carvers, wicker producers, and weavers, respectively. If this employment were not available, incomes would fall by almost 40%, with no indication from survey results that the shortfall could be made up elsewhere.

In fact, actual contributions to total household income are even higher than these figures indicate, because many of the products, especially those made from bamboo, are locally available, thus saving additional costs. Fish traps and baskets, for example, are made from local materials.

Women are the main contributors to this type of household income, but as we have seen in other countries, their role is not calculated or acknowledged, because national surveys overlook part-time employment. This study found that in most cases they are responsible for up to 40% of a family's cash earnings. This confirms World Bank findings on the high level of off-farm employment in Thailand (World Bank 1983), as well as a Kasetart University study on rural industries, which found that 40% of the women in 10 600 households throughout the country earned cash incomes from nonagricultural labour (Narongchai Akrasanee et al. n.d.).

The irony in these findings, however, is that it is precisely because of the strong link to agriculture that some of these products may die out in the future. Craft entrepreneurs often find it extremely difficult to meet production deadlines as a result of labour shortages during periods of peak agricultural activity. In weaving, for example, 81% of workers left their jobs for farming at some time during the year (Table 40). This situation is similar among wood workers and wicker producers, with 57% and 56% leaving, respectively. Land preparation, harvesting, and threshing constantly interrupt entrepreneurs' plans for meeting production deadlines. This is also a serious constraint for entrepreneurs who wish to expand. Any entrepreneur in this region who wants to penetrate the export market, for example, where large volumes and punctual deliveries are essential, will find this labour shortage difficult to overcome.

Table 40. Reasons reported by craft workers (%) for work disruption.

	Agriculture	Festivals	Illness	Personal affairs
Weavers				
Chiangmai				
Own home (85)[a]	88.2	5.9	4.7	1.2
Factory in village (21)	38.1	52.4	9.5	—
Lamphun				
Own home (49)	87.8	10.2	2.0	—
Factory in village (3)	100.0	—	—	—
Factory in municipality (1)	100.0	—	—	—
Total (159)	81.8	13.2	4.4	0.6
Wood carvers				
Chiangmai				
Own home (33)	81.8	6.1	3.3	9.1
Factory in village (55)	54.6	10.9	7.3	27.3
Factory in sanitary (2)	—	—	—	100.0
Factory in municipality (12)	16.7	—	25.0	58.3
Lamphun				
Own home (7)	42.9	—	14.3	42.9
Factory in village (6)	66.7	—	16.7	16.7
Total (115)	57.4	7.0	8.7	27.0
Wicker workers				
Chiangmai				
Own home in village (3)	100.0	—	—	—
Own home in sanitary (9)	52.6	15.8	10.5	21.1
Factory in sanitary (47)	48.9	29.8	6.4	14.9
Lamphun				
Own home in village (17)	82.4	15.9	5.9	5.9
Own home in sanitary (6)	66.7	33.3	—	—
Factory in sanitary (14)	42.9	21.4	21.4	14.3
Total (106)	56.6	21.7	8.5	13.2

[a] Sample size is given in parentheses.

Incomes

Only approximate conclusions can be drawn when one tries to compare the incomes of the 590 respondents in this survey with statistics for the upper northern region. This is due to the unavailability of data for similar years, as well as different methods of calculation. For example, data from the Ministry of Agriculture for 1978–79 show total household income in the upper north to be THB 14 021 (World Bank 1983, p. 166). Another study among 121 households in the same region during 1980–81 found that total household income fluctuated between THB 24 751 and THB 33 784 (Narongchai Akrasanee et al. n.d., p. 15), figures substantially higher than those reported for 1978–79 by the Ministry of Agriculture. In this research project, conducted in 1984, average household income was THB 26 934. Two conclusions can be drawn from these divergent figures. The most obvious one is the need for systematic time series data, which would allow meaningful policy conclusions to be drawn. Second, however, is the fact that Thai villages are fairly heterogeneous and complex with respect to their sources of income. Government efforts to improve village welfare must be very specific in their orientation.

When looking at wage rates (Table 39), two points should be noted. First, compared with previously published data, wages reported here show little improvement over time, given increases in the consumer price index. In 1979–80, daily rural wage rates for the north were estimated at THB 31 (ILO–ARTEP 1985, p. 48). This study found that daily wages were THB 48, 44, and 25 for bamboo, wood, and cotton, respectively. These 1984 figures in each case were below the legally stipulated wage rate of THB 65 per day in Chiangmai and THB 59 per day in Lamphun. Therefore, although craft income represents an important part of household earnings, the returns are very low and clearly act as a disincentive to growth. Despite this, artisans remain in the trade, due to the lack of alternative employment opportunities, lack of information, and difficulty in transferring skills.

Demand

In all three craft industries studied, entrepreneurs are contending with stiff competition from other exporting countries, as well as with factory substitutes. Wood products are oriented mainly toward tourist and export markets, and research shows that quality is a more important factor than price in determining sales. The competition from neighbouring Asian countries is keen, but high quality craftsmanship has kept Thai products competitive. However, there are two areas of concern: other countries have been able to upgrade their technology more quickly, giving them an edge in price; also, field surveys show that too many entrepreneurs do not cure their wood sufficiently, and this has led to some loss of sales.

In wicker exports, Thailand finds that it is losing out to China, which now supplies 25% of U.S. demand, as against 1% from Thailand. Taiwan and the Philippines are also major competitors. In utilitarian products, rural producers must contend with factory substitutes, which have made inroads into their markets. For rural artisans making goods on a small-scale basis primarily for local use, the future is doubtful. More optimistic reports come from larger scale entrepreneurs who have diversified their product lines and cater to more than one market.

Woven goods face a similar situation to that of wicker. Sales have been affected by factory goods, which are 20% cheaper and come in standardized sizes. Commercial buyers purchase hand-woven cloth for its novelty and cater to tourists and the export market. However, the future for local domestic consumption is not bright.

Subcontracting

Almost all sales to entrepreneurs of wicker and cotton are through subcontracting. (For research results on subcontracting arrangements among a variety of rural industries, see Meads (1981).) Competition from agriculture is again a major reason why entrepreneurs will not invest in workshops or factories which would remain idle when workers leave for farming. Furthermore, subcontracting allows entrepreneurs to avoid Labour Department regulations on minimum wages and social benefits.

Disadvantages to subcontracting, however, are loss of quality and pilfering, due to a lack of supervision. In the cotton industry, for example, it is common for workers to weave cloth more loosely than required. Leftover yarn is then available to be sold privately. This practice not only increases the cost of production, which is passed on to the consumer, but also lowers quality. To counteract the problem, some entrepreneurs are now weighing raw materials before distribution and again when the goods are finished.

Quality

Each of the three groups of products studied has quality control problems. For cotton and wicker goods, the rural production base, lack of supervision, and the use of simple technologies have resulted in goods that are often difficult to market outside the immediate area. Cotton textiles, for example, commonly shrink and colours run. As discussed, manufacturing in a centralized location is avoided by entrepreneurs, due to unacceptably high investment and overhead costs. Given this reality, the markets for wicker and cotton will have to expand significantly before there can be any real improvement in quality.

Raw Material Supplies

Although there are occasional shortages of wicker and cotton, this is not a key constraint, unlike the situation for teak, where the very future of the industry is threatened by the lack of a secure supply. Among the teak entrepreneurs questioned, 38% replied that future expansion is impossible due to the lack of supply. This percentage will no doubt increase over time.

The problems involved in supplying teak highlight the dilemma faced by a government trying to conserve scarce resources for the future and at the same time supply sufficent quantities for production. As a result of the Forest Act of 1975, private enterprises are no longer permitted to cut teak in upper northern forests; consequently the supply has decreased by 50%. To purchase teak legally, entrepreneurs must belong to a wood cooperative and buy wood from the Forestry Industry Authorities (FIA). Research finds, however, that only 20% of the teak used in northern Thailand is obtained through this procedure. Because of loopholes in the law, the vast majority of wood is actually secured through other means. For example, one provision of the Forestry Act allows families who live on the border of national forests to own a certain value of semi-finished teak products for household use. Many of these families have taken advantage of this loophole and manufacture large quantities of semi-finished goods that are then shipped by truck to factories for refinishing. Although this practice is illegal, research shows that entrepreneurs are willing to break the law, because the rate of return on finished teak is worth the risk. Furthermore, wood purchased from the FIA is considered to be of poor quality and expensive. In short, law enforcement is not effective; entrepreneurs are forced to take advantage of loopholes and cut logs illegally. In 1984, the number of illegally procured logs was three times higher than the number purchased through the FIA.

Credit

Research shows that government programs to extend rural credit could be improved in each of the three industries. The majority of these rural producers have no realistic hope of access to bank financing, due to the small nature of their operations, lack of collateral, distance from banks, etc. When entrepreneurs, whether large or small, go to noninstitutional sources for financing, they pay an average of 47% in interest charges. As a result of these high rates, 35% of the cotton entrepreneurs questioned are reluctant to expand, as are 35% in the wood industry and 22% in wicker.

Training

Only a large-scale evaluation of training in numerous craft fields could address the usefulness of existing programs for skills transfer. The task was beyond the scope of this project. However, it was found that only 1% of all respondents had been trained by government institutions, despite the fact that three national agencies had trained over 21 000 people by 1983. It is probable that Thai programs, like those in other countries, could be improved. Most large-scale government training initiatives find it impossible to correlate training with a proven market demand for a product. A World Bank report states: "While thousands of villagers have been reached by training programs, because of a lack of follow-up and/or of demand, the skills often fall into disuse and only a limited amount of income-generating activity has resulted" (World Bank 1983, p. 125). As it is not clear on what evidence this statement was made, it would be useful to have it either corroborated or refuted by additional research.

Future Perceptions

Artisans were asked whether they plan to continue in their trade and whether they expect their children to follow suit. Answers are somewhat similar to findings in other countries, although less negative.

Virtually all workers (91.0, 91.2, and 94.6% of craft workers in wicker, wood, and cotton, respectively) who are currently employed in these trades will continue (Table 41). This is not surprising, as employment mobility is greatly restricted. However, artisans replied in different ways when asked whether their children should follow suit. In wicker and cotton, both rural-based industries, the majority still expect their children to remain in this line of work, even on a part-time basis: wicker 64%, cotton weaving 56%. However, in wood manufacture, which is more urban based and where employment opportunities are greater, the replies were the opposite: 54% say that their children should take up another line of work. This is the case even though incomes are higher than in the other two industries.

Table 41. Workers' perceptions of the future.

	Will continue in craft		Want children to enter trade	
	Yes (%)	No (%)	Yes (%)	No (%)
Wicker workers				
Chiangmai	91.0	9.0	61.1	38.9
Lamphun	90.9	9.0	69.4	30.6
Total	91.0	9.0	64.4	35.6
Wood carvers				
Chiangmai	90.2	9.8	40.9	59.1
Lamphun	95.7	4.4	65.4	34.6
Total	91.2	8.8	45.6	54.4
Weavers				
Chiangmai	91.9	8.1	55.6	44.4
Lamphun	98.8	1.2	58.7	41.3
Total	94.6	5.4	56.8	43.2

Conclusions

For rural households in the upper north involved in craft production, income from the sale of wicker, wood, and cotton products accounts for 40% of total family income. Furthermore, the data show that as a result of combining craft and agricultural earnings, household incomes are not only above the poverty line but also above the national average. This is surprising, considering that in this region of Thailand incomes are among the lowest in the country. In short, non-farm income is important in poor agricultural communities.

However, rural producers who make goods for local consumption find that their markets are shrinking. Thailand's economy has become increasingly sophisticated and its rural infrastructure has improved. Factory goods are readily available and cheap. Given this factory competition, high family incomes of rural craft workers will likely decline in the future. From a policy point of view, two things are essential: artisans who are reasonably close to towns and cities should be encouraged to expand the range of their products to include goods for tourist and export markets; when this is not possible, alternative employment sources must be found.

To help producers diversify their exports, something must be done about competition between the craft trades and agriculture over the supply of labour. It was found that 67% of rural producers leave their work for farming at some time during the year. This has severely hampered entrepreneurs' plans for business expansion. This is a difficult dilemma to resolve, given the fact that agriculture is the base of these rural communities. An increased use of urban labour is one solution, although wages would have to be higher. Furthermore, this option would take income away from rural workers.

Craft export sales have increased from THB 213 million in 1970 to THB 8.5 billion in 1982, for an average annual increase of 38%, which is much higher than the increase in overall trade. In other words, the export market is expanding, while local domestic trade is decreasing.

Thailand has found that export competition from neighbouring Asian countries is particularly strong. For example, China now provides 25% of U.S. wicker imports, compared with Thailand's 1%. At this point, we do not know whether Thailand is losing or gaining ground to other countries. However, we are aware of the much higher export levels from Taiwan and Korea. In 1984, Taiwan's craft exports totaled USD 2.4 billion and South Korea's, USD 1.2 billion. These are many times higher than Thailand's craft exports. These figures suggest that it is important to keep abreast of technological innovations, especially in industries such as wood, which require more advanced technologies to achieve export standards. Taiwan and Korea have been able to improve their technologies more quickly, thereby giving them an edge in price.

It is interesting to note that Thailand has fewer support agencies than neighbouring countries. In other countries, governments have established an average of 10–13 such agencies; in Thailand there are roughly half this number. As a result, there are fewer problems of coordination. Furthermore, export agencies in particular appear to be more aggressive. Unlike other countries (excluding India), Thailand also provides protection for indigenous industries that export such goods as silk, ceramics, and carpets.

To conclude, Thailand will find that its production base will move to towns and cities in the future. Exports will continue to grow and products will continue to diversify. However, what is gained from exports by way of exchange and employment will be counter-balanced by losses incurred by rural producers. This is a serious cause for concern and calls for subcontracting arrangements between rural workers and urban entrepreneurs serving the export market. Failing this, additional nonfarm employment will be required, but it is not clear at this point what form it will take.

Malaysia

This study on the role of artisans in the Malaysian economy was carried out to investigate a number of emerging concerns. Although the country had a per capita income in 1982 of USD 2000, which put it ahead of most other Asian nations, the benefits of rapid economic growth have not reached all segments of the population. In particular, the government has argued that the indigenous *bumiputras*, or "sons of the soil," have not had their fair share of national wealth, most of which comes from oil, timber, rubber, palm oil, and tin. As a result, recent national development plans have stressed a more equitable redistribution of wealth among the three major ethnic groups: Malays, Chinese, and Indians. A particular focus of government efforts has been on the Malays, who account for a majority of the rural population, but have lower incomes than other ethnic groups (Table 42). This study is important in this context, because craft employment has a large rural Malay base. Producers are mainly agriculturalists who depend on craft employment to supplement relatively low farm incomes.

A second concern prompting this study was the rapid drop in export earnings over the past few years, as a result of depressed prices for oil and other commodities in the world market. Earnings from export of natural resources have traditionally been the backbone of Malaysia's economy, and the government is now urgently trying to fill this breach from every possible source. However, information has been insufficient for predicting how large a role craft exports can play.

Finally, there are no less than 13 government agencies providing promotion and development assistance. It is surprising that, until this research was conducted, there had never been a national study on Malaysia's artisans. Government revenues were supporting a sector about which very little was known, hence the need for research.

The purpose of this study, therefore, was to cast light on the Malay artisan economy and evaluate policies that affect it. Despite limitations in the data bases, all available census and trade data were examined. The historical emphasis on plantation agriculture, mining, and heavy industry has left the craft sector of the economy unexplored. This is reflected in national record-keeping systems, which yield only rough approximations for employment, although more precise figures are available for export trade. At a micro level, field surveys were carried out among 458 weavers, fibre plaiters, and silver workers (Table 43). Choosing these products allowed researchers to capture the dynamics of the local, tourist, and export markets. Research was conducted in 1984–85 and covered peninsular Malaysia as well as Sabah and Sarawak.

Finally, in terms of a definition for crafts, the Malaysian situation is similar to that which exists elsewhere in Asia. There is no official definition, and this is clearly one reason why national-level data are less than precise. For example, the Ministry of Trade and Industries gives its officers the discretion to determine whether an export product is a craft. As this is done on a case-by-case basis, among people with different points of view, the end result is far from satisfactory. The closest that one can come to a

Table 42. Average household monthly income by ethnic group and by location, peninsular Malaysia.

	1979		1984	
	MYR[a]	% of all groups	MYR[a]	% of all groups
Chinese	565	135.5	678	137.2
Indians	455	109.1	494	100.0
Malays	296	70.9	384	77.7
Urban	587	140.7	695	140.7
Rural	331	79.3	372	75.3
Average of all groups	417	100	494	100

Source: Fifth Malaysia Plan.
[a]Constant 1970 prices. 2.45 Malaysian ringgit (MYR) = 1 USD.

Table 43. Sample size by product type and organization of production.

Organization of production	Silver		Weaving		Plaiting	
	Number	%	Number	%	Number	%
Artisan– entrepreneur	8	15	62	37	95	40
"Put-out" artisan	37	70	58	35	56	24
Family artisan	0	0	38	23	59	25
Workshop artisan	7	13	2	1	7	3
Other	1	2	7	4	19	8
Total	53	100	167	100	236	100

national definition although it is not, in fact, used nationally is the description given by the Malaysian Handicrafts Development Corporation (MHDC), a government agency and a focus for craft development policy in Malaysia. The MHDC defines a craft as a manual, skill-intensive product made with or without the use of tools, simple instruments, or implements operated directly or indirectly by the craft worker. There is no evidence that this definiton has relevance for agencies other than the MHDC.

Craft Employment at the National Level

The Malaysian population census does not specifically test for artisan employment, therefore only a rough estimate can be made. However, seven occupational categories that are most related to craft production were taken from the census information and analyzed by area of the country, ethnic group, and rural or urban base (Tables 44 and 45). There were 128 000 craft-related workers in the country in 1980 among a labour force of 9 million. These statistics are for full-time workers only. Because there is a great deal of part-time employment, the actual total would be much higher. For example, the census excludes 4.4 million women, who work at home. Weaving and plaiting, for example, are done almost exclusively by women at home.

Several points should be noted to clarify our understanding of these employment levels. Figures are biased in all categories as a result of the large number of Chinese tailors working in urban areas. Because these enterprises do not, for the most part, reflect the type of craft products discussed in this chapter, full-time employment would actually be lower than the total reported (Table 45). Chinese employment in the artisan sector would also, of course, be less. National figures would show a more even balance between rural and urban workers.

The Chinese, even when the tailor category is excluded, are located predominantly in urban centres and have a majority of workers in precious stones and jewelry. Malay workers are found more commonly in rural than in urban areas and have the largest number of workers nationally. They are also the largest work force in textile weaving, glass and pottery making, and fibre plaiting. The few Indians employed as artisans are evenly distributed in both rural and urban areas.

Craft Exports

Published statistics on Malaysian craft exports are not easily obtainable, largely because of the problem of defining crafts, as discussed above. However, approxima-

Table 44. Population ('000), aged 10 years and over, by selected occupation[a] and area of Malaysia.

	West Malaysia	Sabah	Sarawak	Total Malaysia
Metal workers	9.45	—[b]	—	9.45
Spinners, weavers, related workers	25.56	—	—	25.56
Tailors, sewers, related workers	55.46	1.19	2.20	58.85
Stone cutters, carvers	1.07	—	—	1.07
Jewelry and precious metal workers	4.84	0.11	0.18	5.13
Glassformers, potters, related workers	11.72	0.39	0.81	12.92
Basket weavers, musical instrument makers, non-metallic mineral workers	14.40	0.19	1.04	15.63
Total craft-related workers	122.50	1.88	4.23	128.61
Planters and farmers	684.73	79.36	138.31	902.40
Agricultural and animal husbandry workers	474.49	53.02	97.34	624.85
Fishermen, hunters and related workers	67.00	12.00	8.06	87.06
Outside labour force	3783.23	264.79	386.00	4434.02
Total employed	7638.41	613.55	848.24	9100.20

Source: Malaysia 1983.

[a] Classification follows that of the Dictionary of Occupational Classification 1980 (published by Ministry of Labour and Manpower) which is based on the International Standard Classification of Occupation 1968.

[b] Negligible.

tions can be made from standard international trade classification data available from the Department of Statistics (Table 46).

Total craft exports have risen at a fast pace, with revenues growing from only MYR 4.2 million (2.45 Malaysian ringgit (MYR) = 1 United States dollar (USD)) in 1970 to MYR 83.4 million in 1983. The major growth period was between 1980 and 1983, when there was an enormous increase in batik textile sales. However, given the country's heavy concentration on natural resources, craft exports accounted for only 0.25% of all exports in 1983.

Exports are concentrated in two areas: textiles and jewelry, which together represent 88% of all sales. In dollar terms, all export categories have increased their sales since 1970, except plaited products made from jute or straw.

Although only a fraction of Malaysia's exports go through MHDC offices, these sales are probably indicative of the direction of trade. (Other data on markets are not available.) Sales figures for this agency indicate that exports are heavily oriented toward just two markets, the Netherlands and West Germany, which together take 42% of all products.

There is a clear need to expand the range of products and to penetrate new markets. Although this picture of a small number of products sold in a few markets is typical of most Asian craft exporting countries, it also signifies that export opportunities are not being exploited. Surveys indicate that 86% of all dealers and en-

Table 45. Population ('000), aged 10 years and above, by selected occupations, ethnic group[a], and location, peninsular Malaysia.

	Malays			Chinese			Indians			Total		
	Urban	Rural	% of total	Urban	Rural	% of total	Urban	Rural	% of total	Urban	Rural	Both
Metal workers	1.83	2.27	43.3	2.77	1.33	43.4	0.65	0.57	12.9	5.26	4.19	9.45
Spinners, weavers, related workers	7.80	8.51	63.8	3.50	2.07	21.8	1.97	1.67	14.2	13.30	12.26	25.56
Tailors, sewers, related workers	4.28	5.43	17.5	31.60	12.80	80.1	0.89	0.40	2.3	36.81	18.70	55.40
Stone cutters, carvers	0.07	0.12	17.8	0.45	0.36	75.7	0.03	0.03	5.6	0.55	0.52	1.07
Jewelry and precious metal workers	0.63	0.40	21.3	2.65	0.81	71.5	0.24	0.10	7.0	3.53	1.31	4.84
Glassformers, potters, related workers	1.41	4.83	53.2	1.99	2.05	34.5	0.45	0.97	12.1	3.86	7.86	11.72
Basket weavers, other production, related workers	3.03	5.40	58.5	2.77	2.93	32.6	0.60	0.56	8.1	6.43	7.97	14.40
Total craft-related workers	19.05	26.96	37.6	45.73	21.35	54.8	4.83	4.30	7.5	69.74	52.81	122.50

[a]Figures for other races are not significant and are not included in this table.
Source: Malaysia 1983.

Table 46. Craft exports[a], 1970, 1980, and 1983.

Export commodity group	1970		1980		1983	
	MYR[b] '000	% of total	MYR '000	% of total	MYR '000	% of total
Printed batik and other woven fabrics	—	—	3 287	11.6	50 297	60.3
Plaited twine, cordage, ropes of natural fibres	498	11.9	20	0.07	88	0.1
Bags, envelopes, bottles, other plaited products	858	20.5	101	0.36	57	0.07
Plaited hats, other headgear, screens, mats, etc.	16	0.4	22	0.07	9	—
Knitted and crocheted hats and other headgear	957	22.9	1 652	5.9	3 466	4.1
Pottery, household wares, and ornamental ceramics	422	10.0	3 155	11.1	4 087	4.9
Women's and girls' garments	n.a.	—	612	2.17	1 066	1.3
Works of art, collectors' pieces, and antiques	245	5.8	228	0.8	766	0.9
Jewelry, gold, silver, precious stones, and metals	1 190	38.5	19 116	67.9	23 514	28.4
Total craft exports	4 186	100	28 193	100	83 350	100
Total exports (all commodities)	5 163 000		28 172 000		32 771 000	

Source: Malaysia annual statistics of external trade, 1970, 1980, and 1983, Vol. I. Department of Statistics, Kuala Lumpur, Malaysia.

[a]Based on standard international trade classification, excludes trade between Sabah, Sarawak, and Peninsular Malaysia.

[b]2.45 Malaysian ringgit (MYR) = 1 USD.

trepreneurs studied have never attempted to export. Furthermore, 64% said they had no inclination to do so, and 26% indicated that they would be willing only if government assistance were provided. This indicates that significant barriers still exist between rural Malay entrepreneurs and overseas buyers. Research shows that the majority of these entrepreneurs have no concept of what is involved in selling overseas, have no external contacts, and no information from abroad on market opportunities. This is a problem that requires government intervention, but there are already agencies in place to provide assistance.

Government Support Programs

Government support for small-scale artisans has been included within an overall effort to lift rural incomes. The assumption generally has been that rural craft workers are not distinguishable from agriculturalists and, that programs to improve the welfare of farmers will also benefit artisans. Unfortunately, research indicates that this is not necessarily true.

As a result of this approach, the government has not articulated a national policy for craft development throughout the country. Although there are now 13 support agencies, their efforts are not coordinated by a long-range plan.

During the course of various plans, separate allocations for craft-specific activities can be seen. For example, during 1966–70 the government invested in programs for batik export and leather processing. A notable step forward was also taken in 1979, when the MHDC was set up under its former name, the Malaysian Handicrafts Board. The objective of this Board was to revitalize craft enterprises throughout Malaysia and to increase employment.

By the Fourth Malaysian Plan, 1981–85, no fewer than nine agencies had been established with some mandate for assisting artisans. This growth does not appear to have been inspired by a sudden interest in the sector on the part of the government; rather it reflects the heterogeneous nature of the industry, which is both rural and urban, and which produces for local use and for export — an industry whose requisites, therefore, cut across the mandates of many different government departments.

Figures also show that the Ministry of Village and Rural Development, which has responsibility for most of these agencies, receives very little support from the national government, in comparison with total plan allocations. For 1981–85, it received only 0.5% of the total budget. This is the lowest of all plan allocations, indicating government priorities in other directions, such as agriculture (21%), commerce and industry (13.8%), transport (10.4%), energy and public utilities (8.3%), and education and training (7.6%).

Evaluation of Government Programs

Agencies within the Ministry of Village and Rural Development are at a disadvantage, compared with ministries promoting the interests of large-scale industries. This disadvantage is in terms of securing government funds, which flow primarily to the medium and large-scale sectors, and also in terms of policy, which puts the small sector in direct competition with large firms for markets. In addition, many incentives given to large enterprises are not available to smaller firms. These incentives include such critical measures as the Pioneer Status Tax Exemption Scheme, whereby firms are exempt from taxes for 5 years if they employ at least 350 workers. This effectively excludes artisan industries. Numerous other subsidies and tax advantages are also unavailable to craft entrepreneurs.

There are 13 agencies involved in providing assistance, with nine under the Ministry of Village and Rural Development and four within other ministries. For some activities such as disseminating new product technologies or providing a network of extension workers, a multiplicity of agencies may indeed be necessary. However, for the most part, to have such a large number of different institutions working in the same area makes little sense and ultimately leaves the beneficiaries confused. This is especially the case in such critical areas as organization of new production units, provision of raw materials, and research on product development. Data show that it would be much better to have one agency, logically the MHDC, assume responsibility for these functions.

Despite the many craft development agencies, the majority of artisans and entrepreneurs surveyed were either completely unaware of existing programs of support or did not make use of them. Especially in marketing, most respondents stated that they believe that the private sector does a better job. Government support to small rural producers is still largely inaccessible, suggesting the need for a greater emphasis on dissemination of information about government programs in rural areas.

Evidence from the Field

Employment and Income

Most artisan products in Malaysia, like the plaited and woven products we studied, are produced on a part-time basis, mainly by women, and usually in the home. Work is frequently interrupted by the need to provide labour for farming as well as raw material shortages. In the silver industry, however, employment is full time and undertaken by men.

When one considers that the poverty line is drawn at a monthly income of MYR 300 per household, one can see that incomes of the artisan households studied are significantly higher. Total household income for silver workers, weavers, and plaiters is MYR 450, 453, and 363, respectively, with craft income contributing 86, 36, and 34%. This is consistent with findings from other countries such as Sri Lanka, Nepal, and Thailand, which show that families involved in craft production have incomes above the poverty line as well as above the national average. Data on profitability, however, show a decline for both weaving and silver, as a result of factory competition.

Products made on a part-time basis constitute an important source of family earnings. Income from weaving and plaiting represents about 30% of total family revenues. However, earnings are not constant throughout the year, due to market fluctuations. In capital-intensive industries, such as silver, employment is undertaken on a full-time basis, which reduces the amount of time available for generating income from other sources. As a result, although income from silver work is higher than that from work in other crafts, total family income may not be. Among artisans surveyed, family income of weavers was close to that of silver workers (MYR 453 and 450), although craft income differed dramatically (MYR 164 and 390 per month).

Data on profitability from weaving and plaiting entrepreneurs indicate a sharp drop in profits from weaving, but an increase for fibre plaiting (Table 47). Weaving has been hit by a shift in consumer preference away from traditional fabrics to cheaper factory-produced goods. Plaiting, on the other hand, has retained its market predominantly among low-income families. Similar sales figures for silver were not obtained, due to the small sample size, but interviews with entrepreneurs indicate a decline in business. This is a result of the importation of plated silverware, the availability of factory-produced pewterware, and the rising cost of silver itself. In short, two of the three products studied have been adversely affected by factory competition.

Table 47. Average annual sales, costs, and gross margins (USD) of entrepreneurs in weaving and plaiting crafts, 1983 and 1984.

	Weaving		Plaiting	
	1983	1984	1983	1984
Total revenue	140 801	104 051	13 299	16 656
Total costs	105 722	85 122	10 487	13 112
Gross margin	34 869	18 931	2 811	3 542

Table 48. Distribution of artisans by age.

Age (years)	Number	%
Under 15	5	1.1
15–21	32	7.0
22–28	77	16.8
29–35	80	17.5
36–42	62	13.5
Over 42	202	44.1
Total	458	100.0

Skilled Labour

One of the most disconcerting findings of this study is the aging of the work force. The majority of workers are over 40 (Table 48). The sector is clearly not attracting a younger generation, and this will have significant long-term consequences. One factor that is working against bringing younger entrants to the trade is compulsory schooling, which is enforced in Malaysia, unlike many other Asian countries. School-age children are, therefore, not available to work in their parents' craft, except on an occasional basis. More serious, however, is the fact that most parents do not wish to see their childen enter the trade even after schooling is completed, due to the existence of prospects for better pay and advancement opportunities elsewhere, and the possibility of earning a secure wage that is not affected by demand fluctuations (Table 49).

Raw Material Supplies and Credit

Malaysia is unique among the countries surveyed in that it is an Islamic nation and, therefore, the religious prohibition on paying interest is commonly observed, especially among rural Malays. There are virtually no artisans who use credit (2 of 27 silver workers, no weavers or plaiters). Malay producers will usually only buy materials when they have cash. However, due to lack of access to capital when it is needed, producers indicate that there are many occasions when they are not able to fill orders. This lack of capital is also a serious constraint to business expansion. As such, it is important for the government to extend its schemes for financial assistance into the rural areas and to adapt them to prevailing cultural prohibitions.

Training

The government has a fairly extensive network of training workshops throughout the country, and during 1979–85, 1494 students were enrolled in eight courses. Observations of these workshops indicate that the programs are generally well run, and that after leaving, some students also receive technical and managerial support in starting their own businesses. What appears to be lacking, however, is an assessment of the number of students who have actually been able to use these skills for generating income. As considerable financial support is involved, it is questionable whether training programs aimed at simply absorbing surplus labour, without calculating the market demand for products, is useful.

Table 49. Perceptions of the trade.

	Entrepreneur (%)	"Put-out" artisan (%)	Family artisan (%)	Workshop artisan (%)	Other (%)
An artisan's income is greater than that of a government clerk.					
Strongly disagree	36	13	18	6	8
Disagree	34	23	22	19	40
Don't know	11	12	15	15	8
Agree	13	22	14	19	8
Strongly agree	6	30	31	19	36
The job is secure.					
Strongly disagree	25	7	7	0	20
Disagree	35	28	25	25	37
Don't know	20	21	16	38	20
Agree	16	28	22	31	16
Strongly agree	4	16	30	6	12
The monthly income is fairly constant.					
Strongly disagree	30	6	25	0	32
Disagree	39	42	23	31	24
Don't know	19	24	14	25	20
Agree	8	23	21	31	16
Strongly agree	3	5	17	18	8
It is a respectable job.					
Strongly disagree	6	3	0	0	8
Disagree	19	3	0	0	8
Don't know	39	19	7	31	29
Agree	27	28	24	50	42
Strongly agree	8	48	66	19	42
The job has a bright future.					
Strongly disagree	15	2	0	0	12
Disagree	32	15	7	12	16
Don't know	21	27	14	44	12
Agree	24	27	36	44	24
Strongly agree	8	29	43	0	36

Entrepreneurial Talent

Research shows that most entrepreneurs have low levels of education as well as low capital bases. They do not advertise widely and are not familiar with basic procedures for marketing their products. This implies the need for greater government support in promoting entrepreneurial skills and for training courses in small business development. As the situation now stands, entrepreneurs are not equipped to improve their products substantially or to penetrate new markets. These are key reasons why the craft sector has not taken full advantage of overseas markets, certainly not to the extent that many neighbouring countries have. As indicated earlier, 86% of all entrepreneurs have never exported, and 64% say that they have no inclination to do so.

Most entrepreneurs have a rather negative perception of their own work and believe that their future prospects are not bright (Table 49). Interestingly, the perception of workers in all other categories is completely the opposite. Aside from the factors stated above, two other reasons may account for this. First, entrepreneurs assume all financial risks and are, therefore, more vulnerable. Second, and perhaps unique to the Malaysian context, is the Islamic teaching that a job is ordained. Because

Islam has a strong base in the rural areas where most small artisans live, workers have an overall feeling of job satisfaction. Entrepreneurs, on the other hand, are more urban based and, given their exposure to a wider segment of society, perhaps feel that their work is less divinely inspired.

Demand

Total annual sales for the three products studied were estimated at a very substantial MYR 76 million (Table 50). As confirmed by other findings, silver has a low share of the market and has been affected by competition from pewter, particularly Selangor pewter, which is produced on a large scale and uses sophisticated production and marketing techniques.

A finding of major importance, however, and one that policy can rectify, is the very low share of the market accounted for by tourists. Although 2.3 million tourists visited Malaysia in 1984, they spent only MYR 12.7 million, or MYR 5.5 per person, on all three craft products combined (Table 50).

A number of factors may account for this. About 78% of all visitors come from Singapore and Thailand. In both of these countries craft products are readily available, and their diversity is much greater than in Malaysia. Second, Asian tourists in general spend less on local crafts than visitors from Europe or North America. Third, Malaysia does not have an international craft image of the type built up over the years by India and Thailand, for example. Given these findings, policy should target Japanese, Australian, American, and European tourists as buyers with higher purchasing power and a great deal more interest in local artisan products.

Subcontracting

In general, the "putting out" system is preferred by workers, due to low risk levels: there are guaranteed buyers for products. This advantage compensates for the fact that they receive no employment benefits, lower returns, and no control over marketing or production.

Benefits

One of the reasons why this sector does not attract many new entrants, especially among the young, is that workers receive no benefits. This is in contrast to government

Table 50. Annual craft sales within the country, by market and craft type, 1984.

	Annual sales (USD)			
	Silver	Weaving	Plaiting	Total
Local market (including local agents)	2 729 544 (33)[a]	13 024 554 (33)	13 374 144 (48)	29 128 242
National market (including government agencies and royal households)	5 293 661 (64)	20 128 856 (51)	8 358 840 (30)	33 781 357
Foreign tourists	248 140 (3)	6 314 935 (16)	6 129 816 (22)	12 692 891
Total	8 271 345 (100)	39 468 345 (100)	27 862 800 (100)	75 602 490

[a] Numbers in parentheses are percentages of total sales.

work or employment in larger enterprises where benefits are stipulated. This image of a less lucrative sector needs to be overhauled if the future of the sector is to be assured.

Observations and Conclusions

Craft production is primarily a part-time occupation for rural Malays, but the income is nevertheless extremely important in raising household earnings, due to low returns from agriculture. Respondents from all three industries report household incomes substantially over the national average. Craft production represents one of the few nonfarm employment opportunities available in rural areas. As such, government efforts to remove supply constraints and to assist in opening up new markets are important. Even in Malaysia, which has relatively high per capita income, craft production remains an important issue.

There does not appear to be a long-range national strategy guiding government investment in this sector. The ultimate objectives for promoting craft production, or the relative weights given these various objectives, are unclear. What is obvious is that government investments have been guided over the years by an ideology that assumes that improving rural incomes in general will also result in higher incomes for artisans. Less than satisfactory results have come from such blanket policies. It is only recently, with the proliferation of government agencies assigned to assist the craft sector, that a slight change in emphasis can be seen.

By 1986, there were no less than 13 government agencies providing support to the craft sector. Although budget allocations for these agencies remain small, Malaysia is one of the few countries in Asia, along with India and Thailand, that has a government institution (MHDC) whose sole responsibility is to work in this sector. The government should be commended for this.

As field data show, however, there is room for improvement. Although the government has been active in training entrepreneurs, organizing new production units, distributing raw material supplies, and assisting in marketing, the majority of artisans either are not aware of these government programs or do not use them. This is the result of inadequate information dissemination; a lack of coordination between government agencies and field officers carrying out similar tasks; and the physical distance between rural artisans and support programs located in towns and cities.

One of the foremost problems is the aging of the work force. Most artisans are over 40, and the trade is clearly not attracting a younger generation. If this continues to be the case, it will be extremely difficult to replenish these skills in the future should demand increase substantially.

As a result of more lucrative opportunities elsewhere, the gradual takeover of this sector by younger artisans has not materialized. Furthermore, the national image of the craft trades in Malaysia does not compare favourably with employment in the formal sector. This is a problem shared by some other countries, notably Sri Lanka, and it is a difficult one to resolve. However, it is clear that unless measures are taken to rectify this, the country's pool of skilled artisans will disappear over time.

Because of the cultural prohibition on paying interest, rural entrepreneurs rely on personal savings for investment and business expansion. This results in a low level of capitalization and is a serious constraint to growth. As such, government intervention is required to assist in new capital formation, in a way that is culturally acceptable to rural Malay entrepreneurs.

Research shows that the majority of entrepreneurs have little technical expertise for exploiting new markets. This is particularly true of the export sector: most respondents have never exported and do not plan to export. Identifying new entrepreneurial talent and fostering it should be key objectives.

Finally, given the relatively small population base, demand must cater in a substantial way to foreign tourists and exports. Although most of Malaysia's tourists are from neighbouring countries, these are clearly not the visitors who respond most positively to Malaysian crafts. It is questionable whether government agencies have effectively promoted Malaysian products among Japanese, Australian, North American, and European visitors. These tourists currently represent a small proportion of craft purchasers.

The existing level of craft exports would probably surprise many policymakers. This is because export levels have often been derived from MHDC data, which showed an export level of only MYR 8 million in 1984. However, if one looks at other data bases, one sees that the level is closer to MYR 83 million. In fact, the figure reported by Sanjay Kathuria shows exports of MYR 130 million (Kathuria 1988). Malaysian exports have been more successful than is commonly assumed. However, despite these levels, the market is not being fully exploited. For example, much more could be done to diversify the range of goods sold abroad, as well as to identify new markets. At present, most exports are textiles and jewelry and are sold to only two markets, West Germany and the Netherlands.

Despite the large number of support agencies, spending (in terms of total national allocations) is extremely low. The ministry with primary responsibility receives fewer funds than any other. The key question is whether the sector deserves higher priority. The evidence shows that it does. Field data indicate that craft income is particularly important to rural Malay agriculturalists, a priority group for national planners. In many locations, artisan income may represent 30% of total household earnings. If this source of income disappears, what will replace it?

Craft exports earn foreign exchange at a relatively high rate, as very little is expended in raw material imports. The budget request for MHDC between 1986 and 1990 is MYR 28 million per year. Figures for the other support agencies are unavailable, but their budgets for craft activities would be much lower. This sector brings in much more in export revenues than it receives in subsidy, but is in trouble and therefore deserves additional help.

The problems faced by the craft sector of Malaysia are deep, structural ones, reflected in an aging work force, an inability to attract young people, and a declining level of demand for many of its products. Ultimately, it is not state subsidies or budget levels that will make the difference, so much as demand. As domestic demand shows little promise, Malaysia may be one of the few countries in Asia where a much stronger emphasis should be put on exports and tourist sales than on the local market.

The Philippines

Before the 16th century domination of the Philippines by the Spanish, a large portion of the population worked as artisans. Village crafts were exchanged for products from neighbouring countries, especially China, with whom the people enjoyed a vigorous trade relationship. Among the products bartered were gold, wax, cotton, pearls, shells, silk, and leather. Despite the fact that for the first 200 years of Spanish rule the country served as an important transshipment point for world trade, colonialism had a detrimental effect on artisans. Policies such as forced labour and consolidation of land for the expatriate class eventually led to the abandonment and destruction of many native crafts.

The remaining artisans suffered further displacement when the Spaniards, influenced by the rise of liberalism, opened the colony to other European traders in the 19th century. A classic case was the weaving of *sinamay*[1] and *pina*[1] cloth in Iloilo.

---

[1] *Sinamay* is a local fabric made from banana fibre; *pina* is a more delicate cloth woven from pineapple fibre.

Although recognizing the fine quality of locally made textiles, the British commercial agents deliberately engineered the displacement of this industry through large-scale imports of Manchester cotton (McCoy 1982). Capital was redirected to sugar production, giving rise to hacienda production systems geared toward the world market. This continued under the colonial rule of the United States, as did the shift in consumer preferences in favour of imports. Resnick estimates that household industries in 1902 represented over 60% of total manufacturing value added, but that by 1938 they accounted for only 13% (Resnick 1970). The economic development of the islands, as a consequence, became even more centred on the export of primary commodities, while foreign exchange earnings were used to defray the cost of importing finished goods. Because of the inequalities in the social structure, domestic demand patterns favoured imported products, which catered to the more affluent.

In the 1920s, however, a limited industrialization of the Philippine economy began to take place with the influx of Japanese and American capital. Factory-made goods for mass consumption became common although American business was clearly biased toward the processing of agriculture commodities for export. Industrial development expanded further during the 1950s and 60s with the rise of import substitution, fueled by the continuing export of primary commodities.

This industrialization process, however, could not provide all the consumer needs of the domestic market, particularly those of the poor. The capital-intensive nature of the growing industrial base led to the production of goods whose price and style appealed to the upper brackets of the market. However, high capital intensity did not lead to the creation of substantially more jobs; by 1976, industry absorbed only about 15% of the labour force, while over half remained in agriculture and a growing number — about one-third of the employed population — entered the low-productivity services sector. The majority of the rural population continued to depend upon agriculture.

In the 1970s and early 1980s, the country's development strategy changed from import substitution to the export of locally manufactured goods; the most visible signs of this are export processing zones. This change is reflected in the national accounts systems where a new category has emerged. Besides traditional exports such as sugar, copra, and minerals, there is now a category of nontraditional exports in which goods involving full or partial domestic processing are included, such as electronic components and garments.

As a result of this shift in development strategy, some of the remaining craft industries are undergoing radical structural transformation. The need to respond to foreign markets has caused several changes, the foremost of which is in the organization of production. Large entrepreneurs, who may have no artisanal background, have emerged, investing large amounts of capital in modern machinery and in factories where centralized production is carried out. The rattan furniture industry in Cebu is a case in point. At the same time, to meet orders labour subcontracting is practiced more extensively by large and small firms. In both arrangements, specialization has increased, and some artisan activities, which were once supplementary, have become full time.

Other changes have occurred as well. Designs have undergone alteration to satisfy foreign preferences and new products are being invented for the world market. Rural-based crafts have been steadily moving to urban centres, if not physically, then at least in terms of the effective control of production, financing, and marketing. Moreover, craft industries have come to be dependent on imported raw materials. The outcome of this export-led growth is an unprecedented level of complexity in traditional craft industries, with those that cannot keep up being marginalized.

Scope of this Study

Research in the Philippines was conducted during 1983–85 on four craft industries, each affected by colonial decision-making and, more recently, by shifts in industrial policy. Hand-woven products and mats have survived for centuries and are indigenous to tribal and rural populations. The embroidery industry was founded as a result of Spanish and American demand and now has a large export base. Rattan furniture is similarly export-oriented but, unlike the other products, is generally manufactured by large enterprises. In addition to analyzing already available census and trade data, field surveys were carried out on four products in 1984 (Table 51).

Defining Handicrafts

As outlined earlier, the complex changes in the industrial history of the Philippines have resulted in confusion over the term "handicraft." Some definitions are based on the production process, others on the level of capitalization or type of enterprise, others emphasize geographical location (i.e., village or rural), and still others stress the artistic value of the product itself. Some definitions combine these various aspects, while others differentiate between kinds of crafts.

The Cottage Industries Development Decree of 1981 identifies eight industry categories, in which cottage industry status is given to those whose total assets do not exceed PHP 250 000 (in 1988, 17.8 Philippine pesos = 1 USD) at the time of registration. Among the eight industry sectors is the craft industry, which is defined in terms of "manual dexterity and artistic skill . . . that generally highlight traditional and artistic features typical of a country." Included in this category are utility and decorative items that are further classified according to the raw materials used, namely, wood, fibre, and shells. Excluded from this definition, however, are many articles that should be considered crafts. Among the more obvious omissions are hand-woven cloth produced by minority groups and hand embroidery on apparel such

Table 51. Features of the four artisan industries selected for study.

	Hand weaving	Embroidery	Rattan	Mat making
Major markets	Tourist	National export	Export	Local regional
Export rank[a]	14th	1st	2nd	11th
Labour force	Upland women	Lowland women	Lowland men	Lowland households
Production set-up	Factory and home	Home and factory	Factory	Home-based
Case study location	Baguio, urban	Lumban and Taal, rural	Cebu, urban	Bohol and Samar, rural
Sample size				
Workers	97	150	150	168
Firms	7	15	10	15

[a] Based on 1983 "cottage industry" exports reported by the National Cottage Industry Development Authority.

as the *barong tagalog* (the traditional garment worn by Philippine men), both of which are classified as part of the garment industry.

Rattan products, on the other hand, are divided between the handicraft and furniture industries. If the goods are trays, coat hangers, or wall decorations, they are placed in the wood subcategory of the handicraft industry; for tables and chairs, the classification used is furniture. This division is inaccurate, however, as the traditional skill involved in making a rattan chair is certainly more expressive of national culture than that embodied in the production of a coat hanger. Moreover, despite the use of power implements, rattan furniture remains a labour and skill-intensive process.

Adding further confusion to the debate is the classification system of cottage industries used by the Philippine Chamber of Cottage Industries. As many as 15 categories of cottage industries are used, and crafts is one of these. For its part, the Philippine Chamber of Handicraft Industries prefers to define crafts as:

> Products produced chiefly by hand, with or without the aid of tools operated by hand or foot or even electrically powered tools guided by hand, as distinguished from automatic machines, where labour factor constitutes at least 25% of the direct cost of production, and utilizing mainly materials indigenous to the country. (PCHI 1970)

This definition answers some points concerning the use of technology. However, it does not address other problems. Due to depressed wage rates in the industry, the wage bill may not reach 25% of direct production costs. Furthermore, many raw materials, such as *jusi* fabric (silk fabric from China) used in manufacturing the *barong tagalog* are imported.

The confusion over an appropriate definition is reflected in bewildering record-keeping systems. Information concerning employment and foreign-exchange earnings may be nonexistent or difficult to locate. Moreover, available data referring to crafts are often conflicting, due to misunderstandings over the term "handicraft." The industry, therefore, is not effectively monitored, with the result that policymaking is often inadequate.

When problems of definition or classification create difficulties in estimating export earnings and employment, policymakers lack data for suitable planning. The encouragement of craft manufacture currently comes from the government's blanket policy of promoting the nontraditional sector. There are reasons for believing, however, that the industries in this sector are not equally viable; it becomes essential to monitor specific industries and adopt a common definition and classification system if planners are to detect trends within the sector itself, assess the relative strengths and weaknesses of specific industries, etc.

The absence of a common definition and classification system also presents difficulties in terms of establishing the eligibility of craft enterprises for government support: tax exemptions, finance, skills upgrading, raw materials, market and trade promotion activities, labour legislation, etc. Although the present practice of merging crafts with, or placing them under, different industry classifications allows producers to gain access to varied government programs, it does not allow for accurate assessment of the extent of this support. Furthermore, the absence of standard definitions encourages firms to exploit government programs to their own advantage: for example, they might opt for classification under one type of industry to get access to investment loans, but ask to be classified differently at other times to avail themselves of tax or labour code exemptions.

Finally, since several government agencies are simultaneously engaged in record-keeping activities, there is a great duplication of effort. Adoption of a common definition for crafts and other subcategories of nontraditional manufactures would be beneficial, because this would facilitate interagency coordination and allow a common data base to be established. Even more important, the adoption of a standard definition and a consistent and meaningful classification of products would aid greatly in planning policies for specific industry categories and for the broader nontraditional sector. Formulation of a common definition for crafts, in particular, would also convey more fully the government's interest and concern for local Philippine products. This would pave the way for directing government initiatives to the needs of craft industries, so as to maximize their contribution to the country's social and economic progress.

National Employment and Foreign Exchange Earnings

The use of multiple definitions poses problems in estimating employment. While the National Cottage Industries Development Authority (NACIDA) placed the work force in craft enterprises at 43 207 in 1982, the Philippine Chamber of Handicraft Industries (PCHI) put its estimate of all workers dependent on crafts at 726 000 in 1979. These discrepancies are the result of differences in the classification of firms as well as definitions of craft workers. The higher PCHI estimate, for example, is partly due to the inclusion of subcontracted workers and gatherers of raw materials, in addition to workers directly employed by firms.

Employment statistics available at the National Census and Statistics Office (NCSO) and the Ministry of Labour and Employment (MOLE) are irreconcilable with the record-keeping systems of NACIDA and PCHI. In routinely published census and labour force survey reports, NCSO and MOLE provide data on employment only by major occupational and industry groups, both of which are inadequate for estimating the number of craft workers.

In terms of foreign exchange earnings, the Ministry of Trade and Industry (MTI) has no formal definition, but adopts the same commodity code classification scheme used by NCSO. The detailed codes for handicrafts show that included in this category are wood, fibre, shells, ceramics, textiles, plaits, etc., but excluded are important items such as finished embroidered products, *barong tagalog*, rattan furniture, handbags of abaca fibre, and textiles.

On the other hand, the Central Bank of the Philippines has an entirely different system for reporting foreign exchange earnings for nontraditional exports. Crafts disappear completely as a category; however, it does record craft sales in its hand-tallied ledgers. An assortment of products one would generally include as crafts appear in these ledgers, but there are also such questionable categories as "bags of synthetic materials." It excludes embroidered garments and rattan furniture.

There are also problems at NACIDA. Data on export earnings do not correspond with its own industry classification scheme. Instead, earnings are presented in terms of craft types. Consequently, like the Central Bank, NACIDA has no published craft export values.

PCHI export data are culled from NACIDA data on cottage industry exports. In calculating export earnings, PCHI deletes the amounts earned from embroidery, food preservatives, toys, rubber, poultry, and related products.

These four reporting systems naturally produce divergent results. PCHI arrives at consistently higher estimates, while NACIDA has the lowest. Between these extremes are MTI/NCSO and Central Bank figures. In 1980, for example, PCHI shows USD 350 million in exports, MTI/NSCO reports USD 146.27 million, the Central Bank, USD 131.55 million, and NACIDA, USD 91.98 million.

Government Policies and Programs of Support

Although craft production has always played a role in the national economy, only in the early 1980s has this sector been consciously promoted by government policy. The active promotion of crafts and other local manufactures was adopted by the government during this time in response to the failure of earlier economic strategies. In particular, the strategy of the post-independence period, which encouraged agricultural exports and import substitution, was affected by many problems, the most important being low levels of agricultural production and the free flow of imports. After two decades, it became increasingly apparent that this policy could do little to solve the country's chronic foreign- exchange problem, which was jeopardizing prospects for future growth.

A review of economic policy was therefore initiated in the late 1960s and led to the adoption of markedly different strategies, favouring export-led industrialization. This new policy, which has been aggressively pursued since the early 1970s, promotes not only Philippine agricultural exports but, more importantly, other local products and manufactured goods that earn badly needed foreign exchange. Furthermore, because earlier import-substitution strategies were acknowledged to have prematurely pushed the development of large-scale (and therefore capital-intensive) industries, the new strategy of promoting nontraditional exports was to be implemented through small and medium-scale industries that use indigenous materials. The new policy also emphasized labour-intensive production techniques to absorb the growing number of new entrants into the labour force.

Certain observations can be made on national economic policies and their implications for crafts, as well as for the broader category of cottage, small, and medium-scale industries (CSMIs). From an organizational point of view, the large number of ministries and agencies involved in CSMI development has adversely affected the delivery of services. In particular, the existence of numerous regulatory and implementing groups does not make for a clear delineation of agency functions and frequently results in duplication of work, interagency conflicts, and problems of coordination. This situation has also led to excessive "red tape" and has encouraged corruption. Although no data were collected on the level of funding allocated to different agencies, there is no doubt that substantial savings could be realized through streamlining without undermining the government's efforts. Even more important is the need for a critical assessment of policy in view of continuing reports of CSMIs suffering from the very problems — inadequate resources and raw material supplies, and poor product quality — that government policies were originally intended to solve.

In relation to financial assistance, it appears that the numerous tax incentives and financing schemes offered by the government have helped to ensure the viability of some CSMIs. Recent reports, however, particularly for garments and textiles, indicate that many enterprises encounter financial difficulties, due to high interest rates and taxes imposed on the foreign-exchange transactions of export firms. Financial and tax benefits vary, but there is a need to look more closely into taxes and interest rates paid by enterprises that are of varying sizes and that produce different goods. Data on these issues should help establish whether taxes and interest rates currently paid by CSMIs compare favourably with the terms granted to other types of business, or with those given in other countries.

Financial problems also arise from the inability of CSMIs to secure loans from agencies that tend to concentrate in urban centres and that invariably favour larger-scale entrepreneurs. The tedious documentation process required by banks discourages other entrepreneurs from using government assistance. Only larger firms with many years of production and credit experience are in a position to comply with all the requirements of Philippine financial institutions.

The insufficiency of raw material supplies remains a major problem for CSMIs and the country's nontraditional export sector as a whole. The shortage of rattan has prodded the government into embarking on massive replanting programs and encouraging the importation of rattan poles. In the garment industry, producers report acute shortages of raw materials, particularly of *jusi*, which is used for hand-embroidered *barong tagalogs*, cloth, etc., and other items for export. In both the rattan and garment industries, raw material shortages have not only adversely affected the cost of production, but have also encouraged bribes as producers compete for limited resources. It should be noted that in both industries imports of raw materials (rattan and *jusi*) result in higher costs due to frequent peso devaluations. These scarcities and increases in the cost of production clearly jeopardize the financial viability of local entrepreneurs and, thus, the ability of these entrepreneurs to meet production orders.

Quality control and the absence of adequate technologies to improve product lines continue to be major problems. Although international and export markets place a premium on quality and innovative design, producers tend to concentrate on mass production. The Philippine International Trading Corporation's Golden Shell Award, which is granted to excellent product lines and designs, has not yet encouraged manufacturers to devote sufficient attention to quality. It appears that even the Design Center of the Philippines has not been very effective in helping producers improve the quality of local crafts. As with raw materials and other industry problems, the poor quality of local manufactures lowers their competitiveness in the export trade.

Lastly, some comment is necessary about the absence of measures to establish fair labour practices. Although the policy of promoting labour-intensive export goods is in keeping with the abundance of labour in the country, it does not justify the absence of labour laws. The argument that improvements in wages and working conditions would adversely affect competitiveness is weak in light of the substantial increases in the costs of production due to shortages of raw materials, high tax and interest rates, and inefficiencies within government delivery programs. Rather than suppressing earnings below minimum wage levels, efforts should be directed at reducing other sources of inefficiency. This would be more productive in the long term. Although the industrialization process in any setting demands much from workers, attaining both economic and social development goals also requires that the burden of sustained growth be shared equitably by workers, firms, the government, and society as a whole.

The Handloom Weaving Industry

National Overview

The indigenous hand-weaving industry in the Philippines, which supplied the textile requirements of the population in the colonial days, was displaced, due to colonial policies and the entry of mass-produced, foreign-made yarn and fabrics. Only with the rise of import-substitution in the 1950s did the country begin to develop its own power mills for large-scale textile manufacturing, although there continued to be a need for imported cotton, yarn, and fabric. The contemporary hand-weaving industry is, therefore, a remnant that has been revived in recent years, due to shifts in consumer preferences in the export, tourist, and local markets. Programs to promote the industry for national development will have to consider that hand weaving is a small industry and, despite its recent growth, has made minimal contributions to the economy. However, it should be recognized that, as with similar types of labour-intensive industries, loom weaving remains an important source of income to local communities.

Table 52. Data on the work force and production of small and large hand-weaving firms, 1975 and 1978.

	1975			1978		
	Small	Large	Total	Small	Large	Total
Number of firms	854	32	886	1469	61	1530
Number of workers						
Total	1464	597	2061	2964	3673	6637
Average per firm	1.7	18.7		2	60	
Annual earnings						
Industry total						
(PHP 1000)[a]	395	862	1257	811	20183	20995
Average salary (PHP)	760	1542	1165	920	5575	4663
Annual receipts						
Industry total						
(PHP million)	5.5	6.6	11.6	9.5	165.5	175.0
Average per firm						
(PHP 1000)	5.9	205.5	13.1	6.5	2713.2	114.4
Average per						
worker (PHP)	3451	11017	5642	3197	45060	26364
Annual costs						
Industry total						
(PHP million)	1.2	5.5	6.7	6.0	173.5	179.5
Average per firm						
(PHP 1000)	1.5	170.4	7.5	4.1	2844.8	117.3
New fixed assets						
(PHP 1000)	23	437	460	110	5393	5503
Average value per						
firm (PHP)	27	13656	519	75	88410	3597
Census value added						
(PHP 1000)	4002	1960	5962	3507	1758	5265
Average per firm (PHP)	4686	61250	6729	2387	28820	3441

[a]In 1988, 17.8 Philippine pesos (PHP) = 1 USD.
Source: National Census and Statistics Office records.

Despite limitations in data, it is known that the number of establishments engaged in hand weaving has increased since the 1960s to approximately 1530 by 1978 (Table 52). Small weaving firms with less than 20 workers predominate in the industry.

The industry's employment level has also grown, particularly as the average number of workers in the larger enterprises has expanded dramatically from 597 in 1975 to 3673 in 1978 (Table 52). The work force is predominantly female.

Workers' compensation has declined in real terms among those employed in the small firms, while some improvement in real income can be seen for those in larger enterprises. In general, however, industry wage rates fall short of the legal minimum (Table 52).

Although industry output has risen, its aggregate value added has declined from PHP 6.0 million in 1975 to PHP 5.3 million in 1978 (Table 52). Erosion in value added stems from escalation in the cost of raw materials, which has put many firms in jeopardy.

Industry exports have grown from a mere USD 24 059 in 1970 to over USD 1.8 million in 1983. More and more firms are exporting to the United States, which is the major market.

Set in a national context, the industry's contribution to the economy remains minimal, representing 1.8% of the total number of manufacturing establishments, 0.5% of the entire manufacturing labour force, 0.02% of total manufacturing value added (Table 53), 0.3% of total cottage industry exports, and about 0.003% of GNP.

Igorot Hand-Weaving Enterprises in Baguio

As a city of 119 000 people, located only 250 km north of Manila, Baguio is a major centre for commerce, education, and fruit and vegetable farming. Increased tourism has also led to a proliferation of cottage industries, and Igorot wood carvings, hand-woven materials, and silver filigree have become important products finding

Table 53. Number of firms, employment, and value added of the hand-weaving industry, compared with all textile manufacturing industries and the whole manufacturing sector, for small and large firms, 1978.

	Manufacturing sector	Textile industry	Hand-weaving industry		
			Values	% of all textiles	% of all manufacturing
Number of firms	84 020	4 389	1 530	34.8	1.8
Small	75 597	3 806	1 469	38.6	1.9
Large	8 423	583 61	10.5	0.7	
Number of employees	1 465 378	187 264	6 637	3.5	0.5
Small	252 580	10 083	2 964	29.4	1.2
Large	1 212 798	177 181	3 673	2.1	0.3
Value added (PHP 1000)[a]	33 303 546	3 196 464	5 265	0.2	0.02
Small	1 077 856	32 225	3 507	10.9	0.3
Large	32 225 690	3 164 239	1 758	0.06	0.005

Source: National Census and Statistics Office records.
[a] In 1988, 17.8 Philippine pesos (PHP) = 1 USD.

their way to other parts of the country and onto the world market. Baguio's handlooms produce novelty items largely for the tourist and export markets. A small segment caters to the local market, with its production of knitwear and Ilocano blankets. However, promotional programs will have to confront a number of serious problems that have already resulted in 7 of the 15 licensed establishments closing by the end of 1984.

Organized as firms rather than informal household units, Baguio's handloom enterprises were set up by entrepreneurs who, although generally without artisanal background, perform multiple duties, including the purchase of raw materials, product design, quality control, and marketing. Limitation in the background of entrepreneurs has led to a lack of innovation in the industry, particularly in design.

The Baguio industry depends on raw materials, mainly yarn, originating from Manila's factories, which in turn depend on imported cotton and synthetic raw materials. Suffering from the country's economic crisis, the industry has experienced supply shortages, unprecedented price increases, poor thread quality and limited choices of colour, and cash instead of credit terms of purchase. These problems account for soaring production costs and diminishing competitiveness.

There is little creative input on the part of the weaver, who simply follows designs decided upon by entrepreneurs and buyers. Entrepreneurs complain about the lack of labour productivity and motivation but this may be related to the low remuneration and the lack of satisfaction workers derive from their jobs.

Home-based production, while providing a flexible work schedule for women, is also advantageous to the firm, as it allows savings in overhead. Entrepreneurs perceive themselves as paying home-based workers higher rates than factory workers, but this is not substantiated by data.

Technology relies on the traditional Igorot backstrap loom, although the more efficient Ilocano upright looms are also in use. The industry could benefit from some degree of mechanization (e.g., flying shuttles), but the availability of cheap labour inhibits a shift to greater capital intensity.

Hand-weaving enterprises sell their products through their own retail outlets in Baguio, through arrangements with wholesale buyers, mainly from department stores in Metro Manila, and to a number of overseas clients. An estimated 40% of Baguio's handloom output is exported.

Although indicating that they set their preferred mark-up on goods, Baguio's weaving firms are not able to raise prices, due to weakened demand arising from a drop in foreign tourist arrivals and the relatively high degree of saturation of the local market. The majority of firms clearly have difficulty in promoting their products. Thus, only those firms with comparatively large and established clients in the export market, and those producing for local consumption, posted gains in 1983; tourist-dependent establishments suffered financial losses.

Although many firms have benefited from government incentives, policy-making has generally not been responsive to the industry's problems, such as raw material supply. Other programs of assistance (such as market promotion, product development, and financing), although well designed, have been problematic as far as access is concerned.

Conditions of Workers

As an economic strategy, the provision of employment through the development of craft industries is expected to improve household incomes and living standards over the long term. However, the findings of this study reveal many problems.

Workers in the industry are largely recruited from among lower-class, married and single, migrant women who are in dire need of income to support themselves and their households. There are also indications that the country is attracting highly educated single women who are unable to find work more suited to their qualifications.

Terms and conditions of employment were found to be relatively short term and unstable. This is the result of fluctuations in export and tourist demand, irregular supplies of raw materials, and a subcontracting mode of production which allows firms to employ workers without contracts.

The average daily wage of factory workers (PHP 26.16) compares unfavourably with the legally stipulated minimum wage rate of PHP 50.83 for nonagricultural workers outside Metro Manila, established in June 1984. Nevertheless, these factory workers account for a large proportion of household income, as a result of the similarly low wages earned by other family members: 30% of surveyed factory and nonfactory workers contributed 100% of their household income; more than 40% contributed over half. When asked whether household needs could be met without the income of the surveyed worker, only 4 and 5% of factory and nonfactory workers, respectively, answered yes.

Aside from their wages, workers enjoy few legally stipulated employment benefits such as social security, Medicare, vacations, and sick leave. The benefits given to factory workers are generally limited to social security and Medicare. Home-based subcontracted workers receive no fringe benefits.

An examination of household conditions indicates that homes are poorly equipped with basic facilities, workers suffer from relatively high morbidity rates, and have little in terms of current earnings or other capital to raise their living conditions beyond subsistence level.

Policy Implications

The usual justification for the promotion of a craft industry such as handloom weaving rests on its potential for generating employment and for earning foreign-exchange. Although the industry has grown on both counts, its contribution to the national economy remains negligible. Admittedly, size need not be considered a reason for disregarding or abandoning the industry, because every new job created and every unit of foreign exchange earned is important. However, in view of findings which show that the industry suffers from intrinsic inefficiencies over which the government has little control, there are reasons for reconsidering earlier policy thrusts.

Baguio's hand-weaving industry employs a small segment of the area's female labour force, although at very poor wages that do not even reach the already low legal minimum. Employment is also characterized by instability and the absence of any form of legal protection. Furthermore, employment in this industry represents an inefficient use of labour, as the work force is highly educated relative to the skills required. Nevertheless, whatever minimal income is obtained is important in terms of total household income. For urban-based workers, earning supplementary income from agriculture is not possible; hence, the hand-weaving industry is looked upon by the worker's household as its major source of income. On the other hand, it should be pointed out that home-based workers generate savings for the enterprise in terms of lower manufacturing overhead. There are many reasons why the country's viability or cost competitiveness should not be at the expense of the workers; a first suggestion is that the government look for ways to increase remuneration, at least to the legal minimum level.

In making this suggestion, it is recognized that the competitiveness of the industry's products, especially in the world market, has always been linked to cost considerations. Denying the artisan a fair return for his or her labour results in greater industrial inefficiencies, reported in the form of complaints by employers concerning the low productivity and motivation of workers. This, in turn, contributes to higher average costs per product. Allowing a fair return to labour is therefore part of the solution. Furthermore, the erosion in cost competitiveness stems, not from labour, but from the escalating cost of raw materials, which represents a much larger component of the price than labour.

One way of meeting the supply problem is to continue importing cotton and synthetic fibres, yarn, and thread, but streamline the importing process. The cost aspect may also be dealt with by easing import restrictions and reducing tariffs from 43% to 28%. Although this would bring relief to exporters, local-market producers would suffer competition from imported items brought into the country at below local-production costs. Moreover, the severe foreign-exchange problem that has virtually stopped imports for 3 years highlights the detrimental effect of import dependence in the long run. Although imports may be an inexpensive alternative in the short term, the country will have difficulty in developing its own raw material base. A second suggestion, therefore, is that policy focus on building the country's raw material base, particularly cotton, not only for handlooms, but for the broader textile industry. As records show, the Philippines has land suitable for growing cotton. Only with a developed raw material base can an industry such as Baguio's hand-weaving enterprise minimize its import content and upgrade its contribution to the national economy.

Promotion of hand-woven products should be directed at improving product design, especially for the export and tourist market. To date, the industry has engaged in mass production, so that large quantities can offset low mark-ups. An alternative strategy is to produce hand-woven articles of excellent quality. A third suggestion, therefore, is that the industry develop greater esthetic appeal as a basis for penetrating export and tourist markets. Alternatively, efforts should be focused on the production of goods that are essential to a larger segment of the local population.

Given current circumstances, the hand-weaving industry does not merit more than the scarce resources already provided. What is necessary is a more equitable implementation of suitably structured programs. The government could then let market forces take their natural course, with the more aggressive and innovative firms using their resourcefulness to gain assistance. Units that are not viable should be allowed to close. As the pattern from the Baguio data suggests, the survivors will be the largest firms, which have made inroads in the world market, as well as the small ones that cater to the local population. The fourth recommendation, then, calls for rationalizing government intervention in the hand-weaving industry. In addition, efforts are required to improve the implementation of policies for the broader spectrum of cottage, small, and medium-scale industries.

Embroidery Industry

National Overview

First introduced in the Philippines during the Spanish regime, embroidery became a major export industry under the American colonial administration. In the 1930s, however, the industry collapsed, due to shifting demand in the United States and the imposition of protectionist policies. At present, embroidery is a small industry with minimal contributions to the Philippine economy.

In the 1960s, the embroidery industry lagged behind the cottage industry sector as a whole. The number of embroidery establishments declined even further in the 1970s. Small enterprises are predominant, and large mechanized corporations represent only about 4% of all units.

The 1970s witnessed further reductions in the industry's employment level from 6178 workers in 1975 to only 4318 in 1978 (Table 54). Women dominate the work force, except in managerial positions.

The chain of subcontracting that runs through the industry from large to small embroidery firms and the pressure of delivery dates has led to wage-dependent workers constituting the bulk of the work force.

In the 1970s, wages, which were at the poverty line, showed some improvement in real terms. Increased income was most evident among the relatively lower paid, small hand- embroidery industry workers (Table 54). Income increases, however, have entailed long working hours at wage rates that still fall short of the legal minimum.

Beginning in the mid-1970s, industry exports are reported to have grown rapidly from USD 53.6 million in 1976 to USD 138.9 million in 1983. As the major market, the United States takes 80% of Philippine embroidery exports. Industry receipts declined, however, from PHP 169.8 million in 1975 to PHP 80.0 million in 1978. This was accompanied by a drastic reduction in value added from PHP 139.5 million in 1975 to PHP 59.1 million in 1978 (Table 54). The aggregate value added is small, because the industry is dependent on imported fabrics, and the only value generated domestically is that of labour, which is negligible because of low wages.

Set in the national context, the embroidery industry's contribution to the economy is minimal, representing 0.5% of the total number of manufacturing establishments, 0.3% of the entire manufacturing labour force, and 0.2% of total manufacturing value added (Table 55).

The Hand Embroidery Industry of Lumban and Taal

Although nationally the industry's employment effect is negligible, this is not the case in the southern Tagalog region where many households depend on this traditional craft for their livelihood. The towns of Lumban and Taal are particularly noted for embroidery. They cater to the domestic market, but are confronted with problems which require the attention of the government.

With its production of *jusi* and *pina* embroideries, the industry in Lumban caters mainly to the local elite. The town has a guaranteed market, because much of the work is subcontracted by large, Manila-based department stores and tourist shops. Taal, on the other hand, specializes in embroideries using lower-priced synthetic fabrics. Taal

Table 54. Data on the work force and production of small and large embroidery firms, 1975 and 1978.

	1975			1978		
	Small	Large	Total	Small	Large	Total
Number of firms	244	67	311	303	87	390
Number of workers						
Total	1120	5058	6178	1392	2926	4318
Average per firm	4.6	75.5		4.6	33.6	
Annual earnings						
Industry total (PHP 1000)[a]	805	15798	16599	2429	12540	14969
Average salary (PHP)	1009	2750	2492	2392	4022	3562
Annual receipts						
Industry total (PHP million)	27.8	142.0	169.8	6.6	73.4	80.0
Average per firm (PHP 1000)	114.1	2119.5	546.1	21.7	844.1	205.2
Average per worker (PHP)	24857	28076	27492	4726	25098	18530
Annual costs						
Industry total (PHP 1000)	2541	38547	41088	2388	25075	27463
Average per firm (PHP 1000)	10.4	575.3	132.1	7.9	288.2	70.4
New fixed assets (PHP 1000)	284	5090	5374	40	5498	5538
Average value per firm (PHP)	1164	75970	17280	132	63195	14200
Census value added (PHP million)	25.7	113.8	139.5	4.2	54.9	59.1
Average per firm (PHP 1000)	4.7	61.3	6.7	2.4	28.8	3.4

Source: National Census and Statistics Office records.
[a] In 1988, 17.8 Philippine pesos (PHP) = 1 USD.
Note: The 1975 Census of Establishments treated firms with less than 10 workers as small; the 1978 Census altered it to less than 20 workers. This definitional change does not affect the relative share of small and large establishments.

usually sells its products through the town market, as it has difficulty penetrating the Manila trade.

Hand embroidery is organized as a small cottage industry, using subcontracting arrangements. Work is passed on to the labour force through intermediaries, especially in Taal, where labour is specialized by village. In Lumban, intermediaries are not used, because workers come mainly from the town centre. Only one factory was found in Lumban.

The industry relies almost entirely on women labourers. Embroidery provides a sizable 38% of manufacturing jobs held by women in Laguna and 76% in Batangas. The industry's labour force is drawn from a local pool of women who acquire skills informally at home at the age of 11 or 12.

Workers have little creative input, as they are simply the executors of designs that come from specially hired town designers. Home-based work allows women flexible working hours, but this arrangement is more advantageous to the entrepreneurs who

Table 55. Number of firms, employment, and value added in the embroidery industry, compared with all wearing apparel and the whole manufacturing sector, for small and large firms, 1978.

	Manufacturing sector	Wearing apparel[a]	Embroidery industry		
			Values	% of all apparel	% of all manufacturing
Number of firms	84 020	28 224	390	1.4	0.5
Small	75 597	27 409	303	1.1	0.4
Large	8 423	815	87	10.7	1.0
Number of employees	1 465 378	156 174	4 318	2.8	0.3
Small	252 580	80 425	1 392	1.7	0.6
Large	1 212 798	75 749	2 926	3.9	0.2
Value added (PHP 1000)[b]	33 303 546	1 044 868	59 075	5.6	0.2
Small	1 077 856	245 597	4 186	1.7	0.4
Large	32 225 690	799 271	54 889	6.9	0.2

Source: National Census and Statistics Office records.
[a] Except footwear.
[b] In 1988, 17.8 Philippine pesos (PHP) = 1 USD.

save on overhead. Factory workers, who constitute 43% of the Lumban sample, operate under worse conditions, as their time is strictly monitored; many have debts to pay to their employers.

Lumban has a thriving industry, local demand having grown steadily in recent years. Lumban firms have registered large sales and profits at a time when many manufacturing industries in the Philippines are in a recession. In Taal, however, reported sales figures are significantly lower than those in Lumban.

Demand and marketing problems experienced by Taal's entrepreneurs are aggravated by their lack of capital for the purchase of raw materials. Consequently, prospects seem bleak for Taal producers. Lumban entrepreneurs report problems centring on supply and cost of raw materials. *Jusi* is at present imported from China through the black market, while *pina* cloth weaving only takes place in a few Visayan towns, and its trade is controlled by Chinese merchants. The comparatively more affluent Lumban producers have apparently been able to cope with this supply constraint, even as they continue to receive payment from their clients in postdated checks. Lumban entrepreneurs report bright prospects for the industry.

Conditions of Workers

Although data suggest widespread reliance on embroidery at the study sites, examination of the conditions of workers generally reveals problems surrounding employment in this industry. These problems demand the attention of policymakers if the industry is to be a genuine vehicle for improving welfare.

Data on terms and conditions of work reveal stable and continuous employment in the industry, despite the absence of formal employment contracts. This stability is the result of relatively constant local demand for hand embroideries.

Wages compare unfavourably with the legal minimum wage. In Lumban, wages are higher than those in agriculture, but this is not the case in Taal. Average monthly incomes from embroidery are: PHP 337 for Lumban home-based workers, PHP 318 for Lumban factory workers, and PHP 139 for Taal home-based workers. These low incomes are earned by putting in long days ranging from 41 hours per week among Lumban home-based workers to as much as 54 hours weekly among Lumban factory workers. Embroiderers complain of eye strain and fatigue at the end of the day. Aside from their wages, workers in the industry do not enjoy formal fringe benefits, but they do receive occasional gifts that serve to smooth out employer-worker relations.

Income derived from this industry is important in terms of total household income, with the majority of workers in both Taal and Lumban providing over 50% of their families' annual earnings. This is especially important in view of the average monthly family incomes reported: PHP 1820 among Lumban factory workers, PHP 1761 among Lumban home-based workers, and PHP 994 among Taal workers.

An examination of the conditions of these households indicates that workers have limited access to the basic housing amenities, suffer from relatively high morbidity rates, and have little in terms of current savings or capital to raise their living conditions. Workers would choose to leave the industry, but remain in embroidery for lack of alternative employment opportunities.

Policy Implications

The industry's effect on national employment is small, and its export figures, although rapidly increasing, are deceptive. The lack of economic contribution from exports is due to the industry's dependence on both imported raw materials and foreign clients. At present, the only real item being exported from mechanized firms is the service of the Filipina embroiderer, whose low wages result in an insignificant value added. Yet government agencies are being mobilized and large resources spent to promote this sector.

Furthermore, the heavy reliance on Western markets has subjected the industry to erratic demand fluctuations. Recent experiences in Taal suggest that the pressure to export imposes a heavy toll on the industry resulting in low-quality work and eventually a loss of clientele. For these reasons the study's first suggestion is that there be a serious rethinking of policies supporting large-scale export of Philippine embroideries.

In contrast to mechanized processing for the export market, hand embroidery caters to the local market and succeeds in generating sizable employment for certain local regions of the country. In Lumban, hand embroidery is a thriving industry with a steadily growing demand from the local elite, who take pride in wearing the *barong tagalog* and other traditional garments. Lumban, however, is primarily dependent on Chinese *jusi* and on the now rare *pina* fabric; this dependence on foreign sources of raw materials leaves the industry vulnerable. The government has lifted its ban on importing *jusi*. It must be recognized, however, that *jusi* is indispensable to the industry and that local substitutes have not been fully developed to match its quality. Findings indicate a number of deficiencies in "filsilk," the local substitute, which make work more difficult. Thus, in spite of the country's shortage in foreign exchange, it may be well to combat the black market by allowing the legal entry of *jusi*. The costs could be passed on to the local elite for whom an embroidered *jusi barong* is an affordable luxury. In the meantime, it is suggested that efforts be made to improve the technology of filsilk production, so that the country need not always be dependent on *jusi*.

Concerning *pina* cloth production, on the other hand, a closer study is required to understand the industry's operations. It appears that *pina* cloth weaving can be promoted, given the wide hectarage devoted to pineapple plantations. Efforts may therefore be necessary to establish the feasibility of linking *pina* weaving with the plantation economy. Furthermore, a market emphasis on the traditional can shift elite preferences away from *jusi* to *pina*. A second suggestion, then, is that policy measures include a short-term lifting of the ban on *jusi* imports and a vigorous development of indigenous raw material sources.

The Taal industry, on the other hand, is suffering from diminished demand as well as weak institutional support. Taal could benefit from liberal lending arrangements and marketing assistance that would link producers with the Manila market. As the government is not perceived as willing, or able, to help small producers, a careful and sincere approach to the problem is indispensable. The third suggestion, therefore, is that government support for the hand embroidery industry in Taal be strengthened through measures such as credit and marketing assistance.

Lastly, the condition of workers merits consideration, as work in this industry is important to thousands of southern Tagalog households. Although employment in hand embroidery is continuous and relatively stable, many workers continue to labour under less than favourable conditions. Their skills continue to remain underrated in the labour market, as seen by wage rates that fall short of the already low legal minimum. Yet workers provide considerable benefits to their employers, not only in terms of labour, but also savings in manufacturing overhead. Home-based workers, particularly in Lumban, follow an 8-hour, 5-day working week, as well as fulfilling their many other household responsibilities. Factory workers labour under physically demanding conditions. Consequently, a fourth suggestion is for government and industry leaders to look for ways to make work in this industry remunerative, and to eliminate unfair support practices.

Rattan Furniture Manufacture

National Overview

After World War I, which disrupted the United States' European supply of reed and cane, American furniture manufacturers turned to the Philippines to fill the void. Since the early part of this century, the country has therefore been a primary exporter of raw, unworked rattan. The best rattan was collected for the export market, while the small, local furniture industry used rattan of poorer quality. The domestically oriented shops, nonetheless, produced rattan furniture of exceptional craftsmanship, a legacy acquired from Chinese artisans who migrated to the Philippines during the Spanish colonial period. The 1950s signaled the beginning of local rattan furniture-making for the world market, a move precipitated by American entrepreneurs who, in their desire to be closer to the sources of supply, set up shops in the Philippines. However, it was not until the 1970s that the country became an important furniture exporter, with attendant contributions to employment, foreign-exchange earnings, and manufacturing value added. These economic contributions have been substantial in Cebu, but modest relative to the national economy.

Census of Establishments data for the 1970s indicate a doubling of the number of enterprises engaged in the manufacture and repair of rattan furniture, from 304 in 1975 to 665 in 1978 (Table 56). About one-fifth of these are large firms, mainly corpora-

Table 56. Data on the work force and production of small and large firms engaged in the manufacture and repair of rattan furniture, 1975 and 1978.

	1975			1978		
	Small	Large	Total	Small	Large	Total
Number of firms	257	47	304	518	147	665
Number of workers						
Total	1136	2842	3978	2062	8342	10404
Average per firm	4.4	60.5		4.0	56.8	
Annual earnings						
Industry total						
(PHP 1000)[a]	2416	7672	10088	2321	41286	43607
Average salary (PHP)	1586	2623	2414	2519	4439	4245
Annual receipts						
Industry total						
(PHP million)	6.0	32.8	38.8	13.8	169.6	183.4
Average per firm						
(PHP 1000)	23.3	697.3	127.5	26.6	1153.7	275.7
Average per						
worker (PHP)	5267	11532	9743	6679	20330	17625
Annual costs						
Industry total						
(PHP 1000)	2467	21119	23586	7578	98089	105667
Average per firm						
(PHP 1000)	9.6	449.3	77.6	14.6	667.3	158.9
New fixed assets						
(PHP 1000)	130	767	897	401	5374	5775
Average value per						
firm (PHP)	506	16319	2951	774	36558	8684
Census value added						
(PHP million)	3.6	15.7	19.4	6.3	98.7	105.1
Average per firm						
(PHP 1000)	14.2	334.9	63.8	12.2	671.6	158.0

Source: National Census and Statistics Office records.
[a] In 1988, 17.8 Philippine pesos (PHP) = 1 USD.

tions. Many firms have foreign links in terms of markets, product design, and capital participation, reflecting a course the industry has taken to compete in the world market.

For the same period, the industry's employment level increased more than 2.5 times from 3978 in 1975 to 10 404 in 1978 (Table 56). Approximately 80% of the work force is employed in large establishments. The industry's labour force comprises wage workers, with unpaid family workers representing only 13%. Many more workers are employed on a subcontracting basis, but reliable national data on the indirect labour force is not available.

Between 1975 and 1978, the average worker experienced a positive change in real income from PHP 1446 to PHP 1974 (expressed in 1972 prices). Salaries are above the urban poverty line, although hourly rates fall short of the legal minimum. The survey data from this study, however, show markedly lower incomes; this suggests either a drastic reduction in wage levels since the 1970s or erroneous reporting by firms to census data collectors.

For the same period, the industry's total receipts grew nearly five times from PHP 39 million in 1975 to PHP 183 million in 1978 (Table 56). Raw materials represent 44.5% of total receipts; the wage bill constitutes only 23.8%.

NACIDA data on cottage industry exports reveal large gains from "rattan and bamboo craft": from an export value of USD 980 881 in 1970, exports rose to an unprecedented USD 102.8 million in 1983. Furniture exports, two-thirds of which are rattan, have also grown substantially from USD 0.8 million in 1972 to USD 88.3 million in 1984. This has made the Philippines the largest furniture exporter in the developing world, next to Taiwan. The rattan industry provides a small contribution to the Philippine economy: the industry represents about 0.8% of manufacturing establishments, 0.7% of total manufacturing labour force, 0.3% of total manufacturing value added (Table 57), and 17% of cottage industry exports (NACIDA records for 1983).

The industry, nonetheless, provides considerable employment to the labour force in Cebu Province, estimated at approximately 20 000. Next to copper, rattan accounts for the highest volume of exports from Cebu, at 13% (Bureau of Customs records, Cebu).

Metro Cebu Rattan Establishments

Organized as medium and large-scale enterprises, Cebu's rattan manufacturers produce almost exclusively for foreign clients. Only a small segment of the industry caters to the domestic market: one out of the ten firms studied. Research on these establishments indicates rapid growth in recent years, but at the same time raises concern over the depletion of the country's rattan stock, the industry's lack of effective autonomy from foreign business interests, and the government's neglect of domestically oriented rattan furniture makers.

Firms are generally incorporated and have complex organizational systems, most of them started by Americans in the 1950s. These firms are heavy in initial capitaliza-

Table 57. Number of firms, employment, and value added in the rattan furniture industry, compared with total furniture and fixtures manufacturing and the whole manufacturing sector, for small and large firms, 1978.

	Manufacturing sector	Furniture and fixtures	Rattan furniture industry		
			Values	% of all furniture	% of all manufacturing
Number of firms	84 020	3 462	665	19.2	0.8
Small	75 597	2 924	518	17.7	0.7
Large	8 423	538	147	27.3	1.7
Number of employees	1 465 378	35 956	10 404	28.9	0.7
Small	252 580	12 709	2 062	16.2	0.8
Large	1 212 798	23 247	8 342	35.9	0.7
Value added (PHP 1000)[a]	33 303 546	330 093	105 063	31.8	0.3
Small	1 077 856	52 757	6 333	12.0	0.6
Large	32 225 690	277 336	98 730	35.6	0.3

Source: National Census and Statistics Office records.
[a]In 1988, 17.8 Philippine pesos (PHP) = 1 USD.

112

tion ranging from PHP 50 000 to as much as PHP 2 million at current prices. The assets of these firms have increased tremendously over the years, placing most in the medium and large-scale category.

The firms studied produce almost exclusively for export, with 1983 sales figures averaging about USD 1.4 million per firm. They enjoy a growing export market, and 1983 sales are reported to be generally higher than previous annual averages.

Rattan manufacturing in Cebu combines in-plant factory production and sub-contracting of usually 10% of the work to small producers. The subcontracted work usually consists of distinct phases in the production process, such as sanding, framing, and cane and wicker weaving. Firms resort to subcontracting to meet production deadlines and to avoid problems involved in using seasonal workers. To maintain standards of quality, subcontracting may be done on the factory's own premises.

Seven firms hold Ministry of Natural Resources permits to cut and gather rattan within specific concession areas, usually in Mindanao. These firms, however, channel rattan gathering to one of several contractors. The three firms with no concession areas rely on illegal traders for their raw materials. Rattan costs in 1983 averaged PHP 4.4 million per firm, which reflects the studied firms' large-scale of operations, as well as the drastic escalation in prices.

Production is seriously affected by dwindling supplies due to widespread deforestation. Supply problems are aggravated by seasonal shortages caused by inclement weather and military operations within concession areas. Rain makes rattan cutting difficult, while inadequate processing facilities in forest zones lead to fungal infection.

Product designs are commonly specified by foreign clients, and Cebu firms take care to ensure that design execution is of the highest quality. Control inspectors are hired to check the ouput at the end of all stages of manufacturing; subcontracted work also undergoes thorough inspection.

To produce high-grade furniture, the technology employed by the study firms is highly modernized. Numerous electrical implements are used, many foreign made; a few firms use locally developed and fabricated tools. Leading entrepreneurs, when interviewed, tend to be evasive about their machine technology, which they regard as a "trade secret." Despite mechanization, the work process remains highly labour intensive. Rattan furniture making requires manual dexterity and ingenuity, due to the suppleness of the wood.

Total export sales for Cebu rattan in 1983 were valued at USD 41.6 million, up by 235% over the 1978 level. The United States accounted for 67% of 1983 exports, Europe 12%, Japan 9%, and Australia 7%. Entrepreneurs report stiff competition from other Asian countries.

As recipients of government assistance, exporters have enjoyed tax credits, reduced duties on imported materials, export tax exemptions, and reduced income taxes. Six of the firms studied claim membership in the Chamber of Furniture Industries in the Philippines (CFIP); this membership is mandatory for those who want to secure rattan-cutting permits. The CFIP also disseminates information on market and trade opportunities and represents the industry's interests to government agencies. Smaller rattan firms, however, are excluded from the CFIP and have limited access to government programs. Domestically oriented firms are neglected by policymakers and have virtually no legal source of rattan.

Most firms see a bright future for the industry; six units plan future expansion. The domestic market, however, is contracting, prompting the lone domestically oriented firm to consider entering the export market. Whether the local industry can continue to take advantage of world markets depends on their having a supply of rattan at a quality sufficient to meet the industry's needs and at price levels that will allow local manufacturers to retain their cost competitiveness.

Conditions of Workers

Factory and subcontracted labour put in long hours, ranging from 54 hours per week among male subcontracted employees to 47 hours per week for female subcontracted workers. In addition, workers are frequently asked to work overtime to meet deadlines.

In late 1984, wages for workers outside metropolitan Manila were generally below the legislated minimum of PHP 50.83 per day. Prevailing wage structures favour men over women and factory over nonfactory workers. Thus, the highest average daily wage rates are received by male factory workers (PHP 41.44), followed by female factory workers (PHP 38.84), male subcontracted workers (PHP 25.13), and lastly, female subcontracted workers (PHP 11.18).

With few exceptions, workers do not have job security, although the average factory employee has been working for the last 6 years, and the subcontracted worker for 4 years. Despite expanding markets for rattan in the last decade, firms are not inclined to employ workers on a more permanent basis, because market fluctuations and rattan shortages remain likely possibilities for the future.

A considerable number of factory workers are covered by social security, Medicare, and leave benefits. However, subcontracted workers enjoy no similar benefits. Compared with factory workers, therefore, they are disadvantaged in terms of earnings, employment stability, and other benefits.

Most workers say that unions do not exist in their firms, due in part to the ban imposed on such organizations and in part to the lack of leadership and unity among workers. The few factory workers who are members of unions indicate that these have assisted workers in negotiating for higher wages and living allowances. The possibility of organizing the subcontracted work force remains remote, given their isolation.

The industry is a major employer, due to the absence of agriculture and the limited opportunities for other types of urban employment in Metro Cebu. Male workers in this industry are usually the major, if not the sole, income earners in their households. Women contribute substantially less (under 50%) to household income because they are paid less.

Although rattan workers enjoy the highest household incomes of the four crafts studied, wages are still inadequate for meeting such basic needs as food, shelter, cooking, water, and other essentials. Levels of indebtedness also remain high and morbidity among both children and adults is considerable.

Policy Implications

The absence of a reliable data base is a major drawback in assessing the rattan industry's contribution to the national economy. The industry's direct and indirect work force, wage rates, production levels, cost structures, exports, and value added are not adequately captured in existing record-keeping systems — a situation that stimulates conjecture and allows, at best, the observation of only broad trends. This is disconcerting, because rattan is the most advanced manufacturing enterprise of the four studied in this chapter. One would expect that the industry would lend itself to more efficient monitoring. On the contrary, government record-keeping systems are not sensitive to industry features nor is business inclined to provide complete financial information. That deficiencies are readily apparent is sufficient cause for a government examination of census and related data-collection schemes for better monitoring and evaluation of the industry's performance. In addition, the cooperation of rattan entrepreneurs is crucial in improving the country's statistical systems. The study's first recommendation, therefore, is that the public and private sectors take initiatives to establish more reliable record-keeping systems for rattan and other manufacturing industries.

It is clear that the industry's continued growth is closely linked with raw material supplies, as local reserves have been depleted to a dangerously low level. The indiscriminate cutting of trees by commercial loggers has led to an alarming degree of deforestation. Recent policy measures have tried to arrest this problem by banning the export of unworked rattan, limiting harvesting to legitimate companies, developing rattan plantations, and allowing the importation of poles. Unfortunately, implementation of these measures has met serious set-backs, including U.S. government pressure to lift the country's export ban on raw rattan. The restrictions on harvesting have not done away with illegal rattan traders, because small furniture manufacturers depend on them for their supply. On the other hand, large firms with better access to local rattan, or to imported poles, have not been eager to participate in replanting programs, as they see this as the government's responsibility. Compounding these problems are those related to harvesting and transport.

The problem is formidable, and solutions are urgently needed. The government should seriously consider reimposing the export ban on unworked rattan and continue to import as a stop-gap measure. This latter move, however, diminishes the local industry's value added. A longer term solution must be based on replenishment of local reserves through massive reforestation and rattan replanting — Herculean tasks, in which both government and private sectors must bear equal responsibility. The second recommendation calls for decisive action on the rattan supply problem.

The export bias in this industry requires urgent attention. Protectionist sentiment in the West calls for a strategy to promote the domestic market. At present, only production overruns and rejected items are diverted to local consumers. Although some perceive the local market as contracting, it may expand and lead to lower domestic prices. Thus, the third recommendation is that government reconsider its policy on export promotion and institute changes for the development of an even balance between manufacturing for the domestic and export markets.

The market orientation also requires reappraisal because exports have capitalized heavily on cheap labour. High profits have not been translated into more secure employment, better remuneration, or improved living standards for workers. The industry also relies on outworkers hired by subcontractors: a labour pool easily disposable during poor months, but indispensable in seizing market opportunities; a labour pool receiving significantly lower returns than the factory-based work force, but contributing similar levels of skills. Although members of ethnic minorities provide the most basic, but burdensome, service of harvesting rattan, they have experienced little or no benefit from exports. It is time to address these imbalances, especially while the industry is still viable. Long-term employment security may be hard to provide, but improvements in returns to labour can be instituted with greater political will on the part of government. The fourth recommendation, therefore, is that government and industry leaders look for ways to improve wages and eliminate unfair labour practices.

A final concern is the country's status in the world rattan market. The Philippines has not completely broken away from its position as raw material supplier. Second, exports of finished goods are too heavily dependent on one market, the United States. Third, despite the existence of the Chamber of Furniture Industries of the Philippines, which aims to protect local manufacturers, the industry remains vulnerable to Western business interests, which have established a local foothold through investment, exclusive subcontracting arrangements, and imposition of product designs. Although these may have been valuable at a certain stage of development, the local industry's continuing lack of autonomy is a handicap. The Philippines must, therefore, seek to establish a genuine transformation of its role in the world rattan market. Considering that other Asian countries have succeeded in imposing tariff duties on raw rattan exports, the Philippines must stop exporting unworked rattan. In dealing with Western importing countries, multilateral agreements with other Asian rattan-producing states can collectively yield results. In addition, the industry can diversify its foreign markets, and the government might consider measures to limit foreign participation. The last recommendation, therefore, is that the Philippines strengthen its position by discouraging exports of unworked rattan, by diversifying its overseas markets, and by regulating foreign participation.

Mat-Making Industry

National Overview

Mat weaving is a traditional pastime, which provides goods for home and farm use and supplements incomes. The industry continues to provide full and part-time employment, since there remains an effective demand from those at low income levels who cannot afford more expensive alternatives. The industry has also expanded into novelty items for export, further stimulating production and employment. The industry's value added contribution is small, but worth noting.

Secondary data show a rapid increase during the 1960s in the number of mat-making firms, from 247 in 1964 to 2392 in 1972. Virtually all are small scale: only six firms employ more than 20 people. At the same time, the labour force experienced an eight-fold increase, from 1200 in 1964 to 9941 in 1972, outpacing the expansion rate of employment in the other four craft industries studied.

Mat Making in Bohol and Samar

Organized mainly as household units, the mat industry in Bohol and Samar provinces produces goods primarily for the low-income domestic market. In the 1950s and 1960s, however, Bohol firms began to cater to the export market, with raffia rolls used for wall paneling in the United States and for packing tobacco and similar export items. Since then, Bohol's industry has not received additional impetus, but Samar firms have flourished with the growing popularity of embroidered mats, particularly those made in Basey. The summary that follows highlights the different production and marketing conditions in the two provinces.

There are only three large-scale manufacturing establishments in the two provinces, located in the more accessible and commercially active towns of Inabanga (Bohol) and Basey (Samar). Two weavers' associations have been organized by government workers in Basey for credit extension. Nonetheless, the majority of artisans work independently at home.

The industries in Bohol and Samar rely on grass and leaves from palm trees such as *ticug*, which is bought from Leyte Province. There are problems in *ticug* supply, because the fields where they grow are also used for intensive rice cultivation.

The mat-making process is manual, tedious, and inefficient. Weavers and entrepreneurs, however, do not have viable or affordable alternatives. The result is a poor-quality weave that does not conform to standard sizes. The dyeing process also leaves much to be desired; standard measures are not used, and weavers try to economize on dyes. Nevertheless, in the factories of Basey and Inabanga, good quality products have been produced, due to close supervision of the work process.

Recent diversification of product lines has increased sales in Metro Manila and to the middle class. On the whole, about 53% of mat production in Bohol and Samar is geared to the domestic market, 38% is exported, and only about 9% is sold to tourists.

Entrepreneurs identify the following marketing problems: insufficient information; transport and travel difficulties; and the low demand for and low price of their products. On the supply side, product development, financing, supplies, and quality control are dominant problems. However, entrepreneurs generally view the industry as having a bright future. Domestic demand for novelty products has been steadily growing, although traders who deal in utilitarian goods see demand trends less positively.

Government agencies have extended assistance to only about one half of the entrepreneurs, mainly for credit and market promotion. However, individual household producers and small traders have not benefited.

Socioeconomic Conditions of Workers

There is a noticeable absence of women under 40 in the craft, due to low salaries and heavy out-migration of local residents. Earnings vary considerably, because of differences in working hours and wage rates. Factory employees in Samar net a much higher PHP 366 per month than Bohol's factory workers at PHP 219 per month; home-based weavers earn an average of PHP 132.70 per month in Samar and PHP 97.73 per month in Bohol.

On average, home-based workers have been in their trade 16 to 20 years and indicate little fluctuation in workloads. This stability is partly derived from the constant demand for the products, although it should be noted that weaving constitutes only a part-time activity for home-based workers. Greater fluctuations in workloads are observed among the full-time factory workers, due to variations in the timing and volume of orders. Although facing greater risks of production slowdowns and consequent layoffs, factory workers also enjoy higher returns.

Compared with their counterparts in other crafts, fewer factory workers report entitlement to legislated benefits, because the few mat-weaving factories in these provinces are new and small scale.

There are positive indications of developing worker associations. Already, one firm plans to organize along cooperative lines, while many home-based workers are members of mutual-aid or savings groups. On the whole, respondents view these collective efforts as beneficial, inasmuch as they assure raw material supplies and financial assistance.

This industry is an important source of employment and income for home-based workers, in view of the households' minimal earnings from agriculture. In Samar, farming is estimated to provide about half of total household income; the remaining half is derived from weaving. In Bohol, rice and coconut farming are even less productive and account for about a third of household income; the greater proportion is derived from artisan activities.

Policy Implications

In Bohol and Samar, mat weaving is one of the few available sources of nonagricultural income. Earnings from this activity represent a significant one-half to two-thirds of all household income. Furthermore, the work is self-generated, as weaving towns are generally located away from the mainstream of development initiatives. Yet as small producers, the weavers of Bohol and Samar contribute, not only to personal income, but to the economic life of the nation as a whole, by providing low-cost goods to ordinary Philippine households. Thus, this study's first recommendation is that policymakers take cognizance of mat making's contribution to the national economy and address its needs and problems with responsive and appropriate policy measures.

Care must be taken to steer clear of that known bias of government agencies, which favours enterprises that have been formally organized at the firm level. Although the delivery of services to such firms is understandably more manageable, it is important to meet the needs of individual household producers who may not have business registration papers, etc. The nature of this small-scale manufacturing must be recognized as informal and part-time. This does not preclude the consolidation of workers into associations, cooperatives, or collectives, to facilitate the delivery of development assistance. On the contrary, research shows that a measure of organization is needed in order for workers to take advantage of more dynamic market opportunities.

There must be more than a mere 'getting together' of artisans to gain access to credit facilities at discounted interest rates. Groups of village-based workers must be transformed into viable production units, designed to stimulate production, improve quality and design, expedite raw material procurement and processing, and facilitate the marketing of finished products. Such an expanded role is required if there is to be an improvement in the prospects of the two existing Basey weavers' associations, which are close to a financial dead end. The second recommendation, therefore, is for a change in the service delivery orientation of development agencies to include, not only firm-level assistance, but also assistance to household production units and, preferably, to worker-managed production collectives as well.

Village-based organizations may also serve as mechanisms to overcome the traditional dependence on middlemen. Although the functional relation between mat producer and trader is recognized in this study, the dependence on traders must be minimized if there is to be some improvement in returns to labour. Traders can continue to play an indispensable role in product distribution. They may still be the best intermediaries to pass on goods to remote interior towns in the Visayas and in Mindanao. Thus, traders and artisans need equally strong support from government agencies. However, in the case of large orders from Manila-based department stores, government agencies should forge a direct link between mat makers and clients. In cases where a middleman visits a weaving town, but relies on a locally based intermediary, the local trader may actually be performing a redundant role. The third recommendation, therefore, is to seek measures that minimize the role of middlemen in production, but that strengthen their role in the distribution of mat products to the hinterlands of the Visayas and Mindanao; in this way, a marketing chain may be established between maker and buyer that is as direct as possible.

The minimized role of intermediaries in production is also consistent with their apparent lack of knowledge about critical market information, particularly with respect to the urban middle class. Data suggest that the mat industry must continue to respond to the needs of rural, low-income consumers, despite the unpredictable fluctuations in demand and the market's relatively limited size. Nevertheless, the new opportunities opened up by the growing acceptance of mat-based novelty items ought not to be ignored. To take advantage of this market opportunity, however, the industry requires fresh injections of capital and a sufficient dose of creativity to devise new and appealing designs. Moreover, it is best that Bohol and Samar specialize in qualitatively different lines to reduce needless competition. The study's fourth recommendation is that the government extend financial and technical assistance, so that the industry can make the necessary quality, design, and other production adjustments to take greater advantage of new market opportunties, while not neglecting its traditional rural market.

Finally, the industry deserves government support, not only because it augments the incomes of rural households, but because of its value added contribution. Deficiencies in census records notwithstanding, available data indicate that this industry's value added contribution is larger than that generated by other crafts such as hand weaving and embroidery. These other industries may be larger in size, but their value added is smaller, because of their dependence on imported materials. The mat industry, however, has a completely indigenous base, converting grass and palm leaves into items that generate a respectable value added return.

This industry is threatened by problems in propagating *ticug* and other raw materials, as a result of natural calamities and intensive rice cultivation. The latter is certainly a welcome development, but the government could protect the palms base by utilizing idle land and soil that is inappropriate for agriculture. The study's final recommendation, therefore, is that a more concerted effort be made to preserve and develop an indigenous raw material base which, in large measure, accounts for the high value added contribution of the industry.

Project Observations and Conclusions

Several general recommendations can be made on the basis of data collected in this study. Contributions to the economy in terms of employment and of foreign-exchange earnings from crafts are not large when viewed on a national scale. However, the many industries, which comprise this sector, form a critical part of local and

119

regional economies. Their effect on local household income levels is considerable. A national blueprint for developing the craft sector does not exist. It is not clear what the objectives are for promoting this sector as a whole or the individual industries within it, many of which vary considerably in their supply constraints, production arrangements, and market orientation. The absence of long-range plans for this sector has resulted in duplication of effort and, on occasion, substantial public investment in industries with little value added return.

Surprisingly, although the Philippines has a much larger craft sector than either Malaysia or Sri Lanka, for example, it does not have a single government agency charged with sole responsibility for this part of the economy. This also contrasts with the situation in neighbouring Thailand and India. In the Philippines, responsibility is assumed by many agencies working across the cottage, small, and medium-scale industrial sector. In general, their efforts are poorly coordinated.

The country does have private sector associations (such as the Philippine Chamber of Handicraft Industries) which promote the interests of primarily larger-scale, urban-based entrepreneurs. It is one of the few countries in Asia, along with Thailand, where private industry has formed national associations to promote craft products.

There is a strong tendency among government institutions to cater to urban and large-scale industries. However, some of the craft industries that contribute the greatest value added are rural, small-scale units using completely indigenous materials. In general, many of these have been neglected, while larger industries that depend on imported materials have received substantially more support.

Data collection is carried out by various government agencies active in this field, with each one using a different definition. This has resulted in widely divergent estimates of contributions to the national economy for both employment and trade earnings. It has also resulted in an inefficient record-keeping system. In short, the data system does not support sound planning, and policymakers have therefore not been provided with the information they require to guide this sector in a wise manner.

In some cases, increased wages would lead to improved returns, as a result of greater worker satisfaction and productivity. As it is, wages are kept low to reduce costs. However, costs escalate more as a result of raw material shortages and inherent inefficiencies in government supply programs. Both workers and employers would benefit if salaries were increased at least to the legal minimum level.

Although reducing import duties on raw materials would result in short-term gains, in the long run the country must develop its own raw material base. For example, there is no need to import cotton, when suitable land for growing it is already available. In the rattan industry, serious problems resulting from deforestation must be addressed with a ban on the export of unfinished poles. In embroidery, substitutes for *jusi* must be developed to decrease the country's reliance on illegal imports from China. In three of the four products studied, the irregular supply of materials represents a potentially crippling constraint to future growth.

For too long the private sector has emphasized mass production to compensate for low markups. This has led to poor quality and a consequent inability to exploit fully foreign markets. There is an urgent need to pay more attention to product development and quality control.

Subcontracting is well entrenched in each of the products studied. This has allowed rural entrepreneurs to expand their market horizons outside their immediate locale. However, subcontracted workers are almost always without formal employment contracts and receive no fringe benefits. In this respect, they are at a disadvantage when compared with factory workers, who receive substantially more benefits as well as higher wages.

Research shows the heterogeneous nature of Philippine artisan industries. A blanket policy, whether for credit, supplies, or training, runs the risk of achieving much less than intended. For key industries in particular, where employment and trade are important, policies that fit their special needs are strongly recommended. Training is a good case in point. Most governments waste vast sums of money training people for skills for which there is no market. Such investments would be better placed in developing new products, carrying out market research, etc., but this requires careful initial planning on an industry-by-industry basis.

Bibliography

Abdul Aziz. 1980. Rural artisans development strategies and employment generation. Institute of Social and Economic Change, Bangalore, India. [Cited in Cable, V., Weston, A. 1983. Indian handicrafts and handlooms: production for the world market. Indian Council for Research on International Economic Relations, working paper 10, New Delhi, India. p. 2.]

Aguilar, Jr, F.V., Miralao, V.A. 1984a. Handicrafts, development and dilemma over definitions: the Philippines as a case in point. Ramon Magsaysay Award Foundation, Manila, Philippines. Paper series no. 1. (mimeo)

———— 1984b. Igorot handloom weaving in the Philippines: a case study. Ramon Magsaysay Award Foundation, Manila, Philippines. Paper series no. 4. (mimeo)

———— 1984c. Southern Taglog embroideries: a case study of a Philippine handicraft. Ramon Magsaysay Award Foundation, Manila, Philippines. Paper series no. 5. (mimeo)

———— 1984d. Rattan furniture manufacturing in Metro Cebu: a case study of an export industry. Ramon Magsaysay Award Foundation, Manila, Philippines. Paper series no. 6. (mimeo)

———— 1984e. Matmaking in Bohol and Samar: a case study of a rural cottage industry. Ramon Magsaysay Award Foundation, Manila, Philippines. Paper series no. 7. (mimeo)

Anonymous, 1985. A brief introduction to China's collective economy in light industries. Ministry of Light Industries, Beijing, China. p. 1. (mimeo)

Budiono, S.H., Hart, G., Papanek, G.F., Ace Partadiredjo, 1982. Technological change, productivity and employment in Indonesia agriculture: an analysis of the annual agricultural surveys of the Central Statistical Office with regard to rice agriculture particularly in Java/Bali. Agency for International Development, Jakarta, Indonesia. pp. 6–7 (mimeo)

Chaiwat Roongruangsee, Sommai Premchit, Songsak Sriboonchitta, 1985. Contributions and constraints of handicrafts to the Thai economy: wickerwork, wood carvings and handloom weaving in Chiangmai and Lamphun Province. University of Chiangmai, Chiangmai, Thailand. (mimeo)

Gadjah Mada University, Research Centre for Rural and Regional Studies, 1985. The handicraft industry in national development: problems and prospects in batik and perak craft industries in Indonesia. Gadjah Mada University, Yogjakarta, Indonesia. (mimeo)

Gordon, D.L., Levitsky, J. 1979. World Bank assistance to developing countries. Paper presented at a meeting of donor agencies on small scale enterprise development, Berlin, October 23–26, 1979. p. 2. Cited in Allal, M., Chuta, E. Cottage industries and handicrafts: some guidelines for employment promotion. ILO, Geneva, Switzerland. p. 43.

Gusti Ngurah Bagus, Wayan Tjatera et al., 1985. Handicraft industries in national development: problems and prospects in Bali, Indonesia. Udayana University, Denpasar, Indonesia. (mimeo)

Hone, A., Jain, L.C. 1972. Promoting handicrafts: path to problems or road to rewards? International Trade Forum, January–March, 104.

ILO (International Labour Organization). 1983. Promotion of employment and incomes for the rural poor, including rural women, through nonfarm activities. Advisory Committee on Rural Development, 10th session, 22 November – 1 December 1983. ILO, Geneva, Switzerland. p. 89.

ILO–ARTEP (International Labour Organization, Asian Regional Team for Employment Promotion) 1985. Employment issues and policies for Thailand's Sixth Plan, main report. ILO, Geneva, Switzerland. (mimeo)

———— 1986. The impact of economic liberalization on the small scale and rural industries of Sri Lanka. ILO, New Delhi, India. p. 1.

India 1972. All India debt and investment survey 1971–1972. Government of India, New Delhi, India. [Section on rural artisans summarized in Reserve Bank Bulletin (March 1978) and cited in Cable, V.,

Weston, A. 1983. Indian handicrafts and handlooms: production for the world market. Indian Council for Research on International Economic Relations, New Delhi, India. pp. 3–4. Working paper no. 10. (mimeo)]

Indian Cooperative Union. 1955. Report on the marketing of handicrafts. Indian Cooperative Union, New Delhi, India.

Islam, R., Shrestha, R.P. 1986. Employment expansion through cottage industries in Nepal: potentials and constraints. Asian Employment Programme, International Labour Organisation (ILO–ARTEP), New Delhi, India. (mimeo)

Jain, L.C. 1986. A heritage to keep: the handicrafts industry, 1955–85. Economic and Political Weekly, XXI(20), 873–887.

Jain, L.C., Krishnamurthy, B.V., Tripathi, P.M. 1985. Grass without roots: rural development under government auspices. Sage Publications, New Delhi, India. 240 pp.

Joseph, R. 1988. Women's roles in the Indonesian batik industry: some implications of occupations segration in crafts. In Kathuria, S., Miralao, V., Joseph, R., Artisan industries in Asia: four case studies. International Development Research Centre, Ottawa, Canada. IDRC-TS60e.

———— 1988. Labour conditions in the Indonesian batik industry. In Kathuria, S., Miralao, V., Joseph, R., Artisan industries in Asia: four case studies. International Development Research Centre, Ottawa, Canada. IDRC-TS60e.

Kathuria, S. 1986. Handicraft exports: an indian case study. Economic and Political Weekly, XXI(40), 1743–1755.

———— 1988. Indian craft exports for the global market. In Kathuria, S., Miralao, V., Joseph, R., Artisan industries in Asia: four case studies. International Development Research Centre, Ottawa, Canada. IDRC-TS60e.

Kathuria, S., Miralao, V., Joseph, R. 1988. Artisan industries in Asia: four case studies. International Development Research Centre, Ottawa, Canada. IDRC-TS60e.

Kathuria, S., Taneja, N. 1986. India's exports: the challenge from China. Indian Council for Research in International Economic Relations, New Delhi, India.

Kiran Upadhyay, Shiva Sharma, 1985. The handicraft industry in Nepal's national development: problems and prospects. Tribhuvan University, Kathmandu, Nepal. (mimeo)

Linyanage, Sri Lanka Handicraft Survey, p. 133 cited in Marga Institute. 1985. Vol. I, p. 287.

Lyanage, D. 1978. Report of the Sri Lanka handicraft survey. Agroskills Ltd, Colombo, Sri Lanka.

Marga Institute. 1985. The contributions of handicrafts to the national economies of Asia: Sri Lanka country study, vol. I. Marga Institute, Colombo, Sri Lanka. (mimeo)

———— 1986. The contributions of handicrafts to the national economies of Asia: Sri Lanka country study, vol. II. Marga Institute, Colombo, Sri Lanka.

McCoy, A. 1982. A queen dies slowly: the rise and decline of Iloilo City. In McCoy, A., de Jesus, E., eds., Philippine social history: global trends and local transformations. Quezon City: Ateneo de Manila University Press, Quezon City, Philippines. pp. 297–360.

Meads, D.C. 1981. Subcontracting in rural areas of Thailand. Research paper no. 5. Kasesart University, Bangkok, Thailand. (mimeo)

Miralao, V. 1988. Labour conditions in the Philippine craft industries. In Kathuria, S., Miralao, V., Joseph, R., Artisan industries in Asia: four case studies. International Development Research Centre, Ottawa, Canada. IDRC-TS60e.

Miralao, V.A., Reyes, L.A. 1984. Government policies and the Philippine handicraft industry. Ramon Magsaysay Award Foundation, Manila, Philippines. Paper series no. 2. (mimeo)

Narongchai Akrasanee, et al. n.d. Rural off-farm employment in Thailand. Industrial Management Co. Ltd., Bangkok, Thailand. p. 40. (mimeo)

Nepal, National Planning Commission. 1970. A survey of employment, income, distribution and consumption patterns in Nepal. Government of Nepal, Kathmandu, Nepal. [Cited in Sharma, S., Upadhyay, K. 1985. p. 34.]

PCHI (Philippine Chamber of Handicraft Industries) 1970. Handicraft industry profile. Government of the Philippines, Manila, Philippines. (mimeo)

Pradhan, B.B. 1981. Industrialization in Nepal: problems and prospects. Journal of Development and Administrative Studies, III(1–2), 144–152.

Resnick, S. 1970. The decline of rural industry under export expansion: a comparison among Burma, the Philippines and Thailand, 1870–1983. Journal of Economic History, 30(1), 51–73.

Sethuraman, S.V., Bangasser, P. 1984. Employment and rural industries in Sri Lanka. In Chuta, E., Sethuraman, S.V., ed., Rural small-scale industries and employment in Africa and Asia. ILO, Geneva,

Switzerland. p. 111.

Sharma, S., Upadhyay, K. 1985. Handicrafts industry in Nepal's national development: problems and prospects. Kathmandu, Nepal.

Sri Lanka, Government of. 1983. National export development plan. Government of Sri Lanka, Colombo, Sri Lanka. p. 87. [Cited in Marga Institute (1985), volume I, p. 121.]

_____ 1986. Census of industries 1983. Department of Census and Statistics, Colombo, Sri Lanka. [Cited in Marga Institute (1986), volume II, annexes 1.0–1.14.]

Taimni, K.K. 1981. Employment generation through handicraft cooperatives: the India experience. International Labour Review, 120(4) July–August.

University Kebangsaan Malaysia, Faculty of Business Management, and MHDC (Malaysian Handicraft Development Corporation) 1985. Handicraft industries in national development: problems and prospects in Malaysia. MHDC, Kuala Lumpur, Malaysia. (mimeo)

World Bank. 1983. Growth and employment in rural Thailand. Report no. 3906-TH. World Bank, Washington, DC, USA. (mimeo).